LANDFALL 241

May 2021

Editor Emma Neale
Reviews Editor Michelle Elvy

Founding Editor Charles Brasch (1909–1973)

Cover: Ewan McDougall, *Man with Wild Ideas*, 2020, oil on wood and frame, 650 x 550mm.

Published with the assistance of Creative New Zealand.

OTAGO UNIVERSITY PRESS

CONTENTS

4 Charles Brasch Young Writers' Essay Competition 2021: Judge's Report, *Emma Neale*

7 Adapt or Die: The importance of adaptation within New Zealand's climate response, *Henrietta Finney Waters*

10 Rigid World, *Bill Manhire*

11 Rehearsal, *Bill Manhire*

12 Inside Play, *Amber Moffat*

19 Society does a collective impersonation of Robin Williams telling Matt Damon 'It's not your fault' repeatedly in *Good Will Hunting*, *Jordan Hamel*

21 *from* 'Small Plates', *Alison Glenny*

22 serpent day, *Lyndsey Knight*

24 that's why they call me missus fahrenheit, *Cadence Chung*

26 Crossed Toes, *Brent Kininmont*

28 Limpet, *Rebecca Styles*

32 Art Portfolio, *Bridget Reweti*

41 Leaf, Foreshore, Seed, *Kirsty Baker*

46 Paper Crowns, Bucket Hats, *Ethan Te Ora*

52 Learning How to Behave, *Talia Marshall*

54 Night Fill, *Victor Rodger*

63 Suburban Aubade, *Majella Cullinane*

69 Polypharmacy, *J. Wiremu Kane*

79 Without the Scaffold of Words, *Trisha Hanifin*

80 periphery, *Lily Holloway*

81 Under the Falling Chestnuts, *Lily Holloway*

83 Field Notes on Elegy, *Claudia Jardine*

86 Beyond the Pleasure Principle, *Philip Armstrong*

87 John Bender has come to live in Seddonville, New Zealand, *Zoë Meager*

89 Heritage Roses, Northern Cemetery, *Alison Denham*

90 Outreach, *Amy Head*

96 Accommodations, *Diana Bridge*

98 Mothers & Fathers, *Rowan Taigel*

100 One Letter, *Owen Bullock*

101 Selfie, *Murray Edmond*

105 And I Suppose Poems Could Be Miniature Rooms, *Wes Lee*

107 Marsyas Becoming Parchment, *Chris Price*

110 Ralph Hotere Finds his Balance, *Peter Belton*
111 Strange Times, *Michael Harlow*
112 Art Portfolio, *Ewan McDougall*
121 The Best Day, *Sarah Lawrence*
125 Grief Sonnet 1 of 235, *Erik Kennedy*
126 Miss Dust in a Motel Room, *Joanna Aitchison*
127 Galanthus in Rain, *Joanna Preston*
128 *from* Parihaka/Pātaka Kai, *Chris Holdaway*
129 Diaphony in C Minor, *Joy Tong*
131 Devoir, *Tim Saunders*
132 Sixty 1, Sixty 8, *David Beach*
134 Kite Day, New Brighton, *Stephanie Burt*
136 Mr Bananafish, *Caoimhe Mckeogh*
146 Smoking Koans, *Aditya Vasudevan*
153 Politics, *Tom Weston*
154 Ikatere, *Rebecca Ball*
155 Calibration, *Ben Egerton*
157 Unravelling things, *Claire Orchard*
159 Route 66, *Mary Cresswell*
160 Braided Rivers—Water Tumbles and Slips, *Angela Trolove*
162 Night Swim, *James McNaughton*
163 The Garden Party, *Ruth Corkill*
164 Papālagi, *Ria Masae*
166 returning home again, *Wen-Juenn Lee*
168 Racism and Hope, *Anton Blank*

LANDFALL REVIEW

174 LANDFALL REVIEW ONLINE: Books recently reviewed / 175 DAVID EGGLETON on *Ralph Hotere* by Vincent O'Sullivan / 179 JANET NEWMAN on *The Animals in that Country* by Laura Jean McKay / 183 SIOBHAN HARVEY on *No Traveller Returns* by Ruth France; *Wanting to Tell You Everything* by Elizabeth Brooke-Carr; *The Needles of the Marram Grass* by W.S. Broughton / 187 HELEN WATSON WHITE on *Te Papa to Berlin* by Ken Gorbey / 190 RACHEL O'CONNOR on *Remote Sympathy* by Catherine Chidgey
202 CONTRIBUTORS
208 LANDFALL BACK PAGE, *Claire Beynon*

EMMA NEALE

Charles Brasch Young Writers' Essay Competition 2021 Judge's Report

This year's intake of forty-two essays from young writers was a healthy size, and once more, the topics ranged over vast and often forbidding territory, much of it serious and pressing. There were essays on teenagers and mental health; the misperception of humans as the dominant species; the addictiveness of technology; personality tests; LGBTQ+ representation in Marvel movies; Covid-19 and the adequate pace of digitalisation, and more.

I found rare instances of levity or colourful celebration of fields and phenomena that young writers felt passionate about. Perhaps because younger writers are still so close to the dictates of formal education, an essay in their hands seems often to be a critical, corrective tool. By the end of my reading I felt I'd been taken back to a stern school, where all the classes were worthy, but I wondered: did my tutors have genuine passion for their subjects? Increasingly, I began to miss a sense of infectious enthusiasm or lively mischief—the high spirits that can do as much to expose or dismantle inequalities and pieties as a ticking-off.

Last year my main conclusion was that the bulk of entries needed more sense of development or shift in their discussions. This year my general impression was of a falling away of inventive, sensuous, energetic prose. I hunted for the electricity of varied rhythms, a boldness in language, and the close, fascinated observation of the sensory world that can animate any subject at all, and any prose—be it a philosophical or political treatise, the study of a specific historical event, an exploration of a social change, or a personal memoir that digs down into a particular experience.

The topics wrestled with this year certainly didn't lack impact. Several writers addressed racism and the legacies of colonialism, homing in on everything from the reclaiming of the term takatāpui (Untitled, Archie Dunn), to the challenges of living between two cultures ('Cultural Chameleon' by Scott Kwon), to horrific, racist murders both in Aotearoa and abroad. This distressing material was effectively handled in 'A Bad Day' by Kaye Maravilla, a well-researched study of the history of immigration policy and anti-Asian prejudice in the US. Her essay was prompted by the shooting of six women of Asian descent in the US, its disturbing reverberations felt by the young child of Filipino parents here in Aotearoa.

In all cases, this year, I puzzled over the knots and bumps, the scratches and uneven surfaces, the glitches or dropped stitches in both logic and grammar of the writing in even the best entries. I say this because I really want to encourage all young writers to undertake that easiest of self-editing tricks: read your work aloud, or ask a proof-reader to look through your work before you send it out for publication. Sometimes a tangled paragraph, a sentence that folds in on itself nonsensically or a weak last line can be the thing that makes a strong piece fall off a judge's radar.

I want to mention two essays for their lightness of touch, their sensitivity and their very welcome flashes of humour. These works were noticeable for their ability to hone in on an apparently minor—or at least often minimised—experience, or even a whimsical thought, and follow it through its multiple implications or layers. They are 'Eczema' (Jasmin Ho), a memoir of childhood skin afflictions, and 'Sonder' by Fiona Rogge, which explores the wistful sense of connection we can feel with people who remain total strangers. These two writers show delightful promise.

Commended: 'Eczema' by Jasmine Ho
Commended: 'Sonder' by Fiona Rogge

Highly Commended: 'Untitled' by Amelia Smith. A well-organised discussion of the impact the movie *Rain Man* has had on the fictional representation on screen of people with autism spectrum disorder and various disabilities.

Highly Commended: 'Time's Pocket' by Danielle Smith. A kind of hummed song dedicated to the Auckland suburb of Beach Haven, with comments on class division and the experience of lockdown—the latter helping the writer separate their own interests and academic strengths from the social expectations of their cohort at school.

Second Place: 'Generation Z's Catch-22: Between idealism and hopelessness' by Peta Kuluz. An interesting essay that takes some big risks—such as using the rhetoric of speaking for an entire generation. It approaches the painful tensions between youthful optimism and despair coherently and intelligently, exploring the role of social media and educators in creating 'learned helplessness'. I wanted to debate several points in this essay, drawing on the inspiration of, say, the young people engaged in School Strike 4 Climate; the rallying of New Zealanders of all ages in mourning after the terrorist murders at the Christchurch mosques; the strong youth component of land rights protests at Ihumātao; and other examples of young people determined to promote social change. Yet I also felt that the writing nevertheless had fluency, conviction and a charge that lifted it above the crowd. It shows perception and thoughtfulness in its efforts to analyse an era and a generation, and its cogency was the very thing that made it easier to engage with, even if that engagement was the impulse to push for the opposite argument.

First Place: 'Adapt or Die: The importance of adaptation within New Zealand's climate response' by Henrietta Finney Waters. A rational, forensic piece, it makes only sparse use of metaphor and simile, though it uses adverbs here and there as brushes of shade and colour that give the argument a sense of three dimensions and urgency. A brisk, no-nonsense marshalling of facts and sources, the essay displays a voice fired up for change and yet determined to be as clear as possible, avoiding any accusations of 'hysteria' over an issue (climate degradation) that has dogged us now for at least thirty years.

If young writers read the knock-out essays from year to year, they will get a stirring sense of how versatile the essay is as a form. This year we have a lawyerly voice stating the case for the prosecution in a court for humanity, and doing so with an absolute minimum of personal content; last year the overall winner was a piercingly autobiographical work outstanding for its lyrical style.

I congratulate all place-getters this year, and thank all the young writers for giving me such meaty questions to chew over about the balance between style and content.

HENRIETTA FINNEY WATERS

Adapt or Die: The importance of adaptation within New Zealand's climate response

It is easy to wish that climate change could simply be 'solved'. That with the right emissions policy all those predictions of a burning, dystopian future would vanish into nothingness. Mitigation—reducing the gases fuelling the greenhouse effect to circumvent a future ecological meltdown—has been the classic approach to the climate crisis. However, in the absence of a magic wand we must accept that no matter how drastic the mitigation measures, we are, have been, and will continue to be living in a world where the effects of climate change are being felt globally. Adaptation is vital. Despite our 'clean, green' image, New Zealand's national climate legislation dangerously presents the idea that we are exempt from this imperative. Given that the ocean is a vehicle through which the effects of climate change are transferred to the land, Aotearoa, as an island nation, is at heightened risk. However, the vast majority of our substantive policy on this prioritises mitigation. While undeniably important, this marginalises adaptive action. Refusing to 'adapt' our approach sacrifices communities to what it is too late to mitigate.

The issue is not that the New Zealand government has avoided action on the topic of climate change, nor that the existing legislation regarding it is ineffectual. In fact, our mitigatory strides underpin our popular international image as an environmentally focused nation. But specifics on adaptive action are virtually non-existent compared to the detailed present and future frameworks in place to enact mitigation. The Climate Change Response (Zero Carbon) Amendment Act of 2019 raves (as much as legislation can be described as 'raving') about emissions reductions (Part 1B). Substantive targets are identified regarding greenhouse gas reductions, advisory requirements and monitoring framework, laid out within five subparts—something that Part 1C on adaptation is not afforded. Coyly, Part 1C barely suggests more than the conditions under which a risk assessment will be made; it lacks even a whisper of specificity regarding a concrete plan.

As Aotearoa's legislation reflects, the global uptake of adaptation as a climate response has been slow. It barely began to gain traction until after the Intergovernmental Panel on Climate Change's third report was released in 2001. The World Meteorological Organization outlines that this can largely be attributed to the perception or existence of a number of barriers, such as a paucity of supportive policies, existing restrictions and lack of acceptance that adaptation is necessary. Climate change has generally been perceived as an issue of the future as opposed to something with effects being felt by hundreds of millions as we speak. Perhaps this impression of the issue is the reason for Aotearoa's poor level of adaptive action, but it does not justify it. Undeniable evidence shows that this country's natural world is already being altered and the current harms that legislation ignores are devastating.

Since the mid-20th century the reality behind Aotearoa's vaunted 'clean, green' image has only become less clean and less green as the actualities of climate change have continued to worsen exponentially. The Climate Change Adaptation Technical Working Group (CCATWG)—currently the only group implemented to address this issue at a government level—cited in its latest and final recommendations report (2018) that New Zealand will continue to face an unavoidable increase of frequency and/or intensity in a number of environmental factors. The CCATWG identified that these include river flooding and subsequent urban flash flooding; droughts; landslides and other erosion; biosecurity threats; and an increase of sea level and ocean acidity. In fact, according to Environment Aotearoa's 2019 summary, in the past century sea levels have risen 14–22cm, sea temperatures have increased 0.7°C, and the nation has experienced an overall temperature rise of 1°C. Coming just one year after the CCATWG's 'over and out', this overview's release is a sobering reality check.

These environmental statistics come with more than just an environmental result. They come with very real social and community impacts—largely at the cost of the nation's most vulnerable. Those in lower socioeconomic demographics are limited by their resources at an individual level to proactively protect themselves (e.g. relocating out of at-risk areas) or responsively rebuild (e.g. flood repairs) when exposed to the effects of climate change. Simply put, these communities are not worried about a 2050 emissions target. They are worried about their homes and livelihoods, which lie in the hands of the government's climate response.

Ideally, New Zealand's future will be one where the harshest impacts of climate change have been successfully negated. To achieve this, our policy must be fuelled by a healthy balanced diet of both mitigation and adaptation. A viable and sustainable national climate framework would need to consist of central and local governments coordinating to identify and respond to risks of the present and circumvent additional harms in the future. We have already seen that we are capable of the latter through the aforementioned Climate Change Response (Zero Carbon) Amendment Act. Currently the former has seen success almost exclusively at a local rather than national level. While this is promising, it is too little—and we must pray it is not too late.

The Otago Coastal Management Plan, a project put into place by Otago Regional Council, is one such microcosmic example of what New Zealand requires 'macrocosmically'. This project has been implemented to tackle the increasingly apparent harms of coastal erosion in the area and the associated risks to vulnerable communities, such as the low-lying South Dunedin. The plan is effective in how it takes into account the most recent predictions of the scientific community (not simply the most convenient) in an attempt to prepare and protect coastal Otago for the potential future conditions the specific area will face. A vital keystone to this approach is incorporating the opinion of communities such as South Dunedin, a historically low socioeconomic suburb, allowing their needs to be integrated into a subsequently equitable plan. It looks at the cultural (Kai Tahu), commercial and recreational connotations of instigating protection against the specific coastal vulnerabilities of the locality. If the likes of this plan can be implemented and coordinated by local governments on a nationwide scale covering all risk-prone areas, it could be the beginnings of the coherent, substantial adaptation plan that New Zealand lacks. This is not an outlandish concept: the CCATWG's final report identified that we are an outlier among both developed and developing countries in our omission of adaptation in favour of emissions.

Without a comprehensive adaptation response, Aotearoa as an island nation will continue (quite literally) to sink under the impacts of the climate crisis. Our government must realise that it is unacceptable to say 'she'll be right' and simply try and hold out until current mitigatory actions unfold to their full effect.

Cont'd on page 193

BILL MANHIRE

Rigid World

beyond the little villages
another gathering of canals and bridges

songs stung by images
a swarm of midges

softening rigid world
darkness approaching in feet and inches

Rehearsal

the cello spends all morning
eating cicadas
after which it is a happy fellow
sometimes burping
sometimes not

now it wants a darker task
no more high & insect things
no more this & that
no more tiny yelps
no more gobbling

AMBER MOFFAT

Inside Play

A woman with a sheet of straightened hair and a brittle smile waves her over. 'Ash! So glad you could come!' The woman is holding a tray of chicken nuggets and a unicorn balloon hovers above the table. It's Olivia's mum. Jen? Sam? Something with one syllable. Dulcie's hand slips away. She's spotted Harper and is shedding shoes quick as she can.

'I wasn't sure if it would be you or Sven bringing Dulcie.' Olivia's mum pulls out a chair, motions for Ash to sit, no doubt wishing it was Sven. He's better in these situations. Still intrigued enough by suburban Auckland to relish the conversations about house prices and school zones.

After the divorce Ash and Sven each bought out here. They could afford to, with the equity they had in the apartment. Sven planted a vegie garden, got a cat for Dulcie. But Ash still missed the city. Before they moved, she'd never been to an indoor play centre. Brightly coloured plastic and cartoon animals, the smell of bad coffee and squashed cupcakes rising up from the linoleum.

On the other side of the table Ava's mum, Steph, holds up her phone. 'Look, Jess, this is me when I met Cam.' Jess! *That's* Olivia's mum's name. 'Look how skinny I was! That's what I want to get back to for the wedding. I've got three months. It's my fat guts I hate.' Steph grabs a handful from her flanks. It's like she's trying to rip the fat loose so she can hold it up as evidence. Ash's stomach clenches against her own soft pad of flesh, jeans cutting in.

After Dulcie was born, one of Ash's clients sent flowers to the hospital: an expensive bouquet with a teddy bear attached. The bear was beautiful, old fashioned with jointed limbs and glossy brown fur. But it was tied to the flowers with a piece of wire and the indentation across its plump belly never went away. Ash and Sven joked that it was a 'caesarean teddy', made on special order by Ponsonby florists. Ash threw it away in the end. She hated her stomach after pregnancy, the stubborn pouch that hung over her caesarean scar. The looseness of it. Surgery seemed so vain and ridiculous. A waste of money.

Steph's phone is passed around. The two dads at the table go for coffees. The mums huddle closer to look at the photo of Steph in tight jeans and a boob tube, straddling a motorbike. Ash just says 'Wow!' when the phone comes to her, quickly hands it on. She doesn't know what else to say about the symbol of bygone bogan perfection. Steph is nice, one of the mums who really makes an effort to include Dulcie. But she's not going to look like that in three months.

The phone is in the hand of a woman Ash doesn't know: slim with a black bob. 'You're such a hottie, Steph!' coos the woman. 'You will totally get there again. Have you considered Ezy-Contour?' The woman brings out her own phone. 'Look, this is me before I used Ezy-Contour. And after.' She holds out the screen, stretches her arm around the table so they can all see the Instagram post of two stomachs side by side: one flabby, one toned. Then she stands and pulls up her jumper, revealing the top of her jeans, the taut brown skin above. She gives a little laugh. 'Yep, my waist is smaller than when I was a teenager. Even at my lowest, I always had flab there. But not any more!'

'Is that those shakes?' asks Steph. 'The ones you get from the chemist?'

'No, Ezy-Contour is really cutting edge. You can only buy it from a rep, but I'm a rep so let me know if you're interested.' The woman smiles. 'Or just follow me on Insta. I'm @ezyskinnyminnie.' She holds out her phone again and several of the mums lean forward to see, tap their own screens to find her. Ash looks over to the playground, pretending to check on Dulcie. She hates this sort of crap.

One of the young mums with a blonde ponytail and pumped-up lips starts talking. 'Oh yeah, I've heard of this—a girl at the gym used it on her upper arms. It's a spot toner, right?'

'Yes, it's new technology that actually penetrates your skin to eliminate fat cells. You rub it on the problem area you want to target, and you start seeing results immediately. I got that change in my waist in just three weeks. No sagging, no scarring. And it's all natural.'

@ezyskinnyminnie is in full swing. She plays an Ezy-Contour promo video on her phone. Mums are listing the parts of their bodies they would target. The dads stand by the playground fence with their coffees, casting the odd nervous look back to the table.

Ash is relieved when Jess announces it's cake time and bustles them into

The Princess Room. Olivia sits on a pink and gold throne at the head of the table. The wall behind is filled with out-of-proportion Disney rip-off princesses. It's so bad it's brilliant. Ash's friend Sylvie would find this hilarious. Ash takes a photo, zooming in on the princess who's a deformed version of Belle from *Beauty and the Beast*.

The girls are captivated by the Elsa cake with the *Frozen* figurine inserted into a cake-skirt. Elsa erupts out of blue fondant, her fat blonde braid triumphantly slung over her shoulder. The girls discuss the intricately piped white icicles, lay claim to the piece of skirt they want to eat. Little bowls of lollies are strategically placed along the table: Jelly Babies, Milk Bottles, Snakes. Sticky fingers grab.

Jess leads them all in singing 'Happy Birthday', then gets teary cutting the Elsa cake. Slices are dispensed on pink paper plates. Plastic forks dig into the soft sponge, release the cream. Then blue-stained mouths say they are full; the girls run back out to play. Elsa is left in the centre of the table, surrounded by dirty napkins and remnants of icing-stripped cake. Just torso, arms and head. Her lower half gone.

Ash leaves the other parents milling about behind the empty chairs of The Princess Room. She itches to go home. Children careen along overhead tracks on low trikes; the humming and squeaking of wheels on rubber matting is punctuated by high-pitched screams. Ash spots Dulcie, yells up to her, 'Just five more minutes!' Dulcie doesn't answer, keeps pedalling madly. Ash looks around for Jess, hoping the party bags will come out soon. A party bag will give her leverage, allow her to lure Dulcie out.

When Dulcie is in her car seat, belt done up, Ash passes back the party bag into her outstretched hands.

'You can have one lolly now and one lolly after you're in your pyjamas with your clothes out for tomorrow,' says Ash.

'Thank you, Mummy—you're the best mum in the whole entire world!' The bag rustles: it is being carefully examined. Ash looks in the rear-view mirror, sees Dulcie's little face fixed in concentration.

Once Dulcie is in bed Ash does a quick tidy of the living room, clears the dinner dishes. She wipes wobbling chunks of poached egg out of the plughole, chucks the soggy clump of kitchen towels in the rubbish. She should empty the bin; it's so full the lid won't shut. But she needs to get her own clothes sorted for tomorrow, get a good night's sleep. She'll do a proper cleanup after work.

She only has two good pairs of pants that fit comfortably. She pulls out the navy ones, finds her vintage cream shirt. She'd be a size smaller without that little pad of fat, could wear all her old clothes. Ash lays out the clothes and flops on her bed, scrolls through her notifications. She's been added into a message group called 'Ezy-Contour info' with some of the other school mums.

> Hi lovely ladies!! It was so nice to chat today and share my success with Ezy-Contour! I know some of you wanted to learn more so here are some links that will show you how truly life changing Ezy-Contour can be!! You CAN have the body you want!!!

There are three links and a flurry of emojis and kisses from Mel, AKA @ezyskinnyminnie. Ash groans and takes a screenshot, starts a message to Sylvie: *So this is what happens when you go to kids' parties in the burbs—kill me now!* Then she clicks on the first link.

The before and after shots are interspersed with testimonials. A busty woman with impossibly thin arms weeps with joy about her newfound confidence. A mother pushes her toddler twins on swings, back turned to the camera and declares, 'Life is great now I'm back in size 8!' Then a doctor talks about how Ezy-Contour is the first of its kind, a revolutionary but completely natural way to eradicate unwanted fat deposits. Developed in a prestigious lab in the Netherlands, Ezy-Contour allows humans to harness the power of the *Hirudo adipolis*, a tiny organism found in coconut trees.

Ash goes through all the links, then does a Google search for *Hirudo adipolis*. There is an article evaluating the efficacy of the organism for medically supervised weight reduction:

> *Hirudo adipolis* have been used therapeutically for weight loss in humans. Vegetable oil infused with dormant *Hirudo adipolis* eggs has proven an effective delivery mechanism. On contact with human skin, the warmth of the body triggers the eggs to hatch. The *Hirudo adipolis* larvae then burrow into the skin in search of their food source: fat.

So repulsive. Ash pinches her loose tummy. That's repulsive too.

She doesn't send the message to Sylvie. She sends one to Mel instead. They arrange for Mel to come to her house after school drop-off—Ash doesn't want Dulcie to have any idea that something like Ezy-Contour exists.

She buys the starter pack: a small jar of Ezy-Contour oil that has to be kept in the fridge, a pair of application gloves, a removal clamp and a disposal box. She cringes when Mel explains how the deposits are removed, but Mel is reassuring, insists it's easy.

Dulcie is at Sven's. Ash rubs the oil on after a bath, like Mel instructed. It tingles going on, a bit like an exfoliating scrub. She lies on her bed and watches crap on her phone as it dries off. After twenty minutes the sensation intensifies to prickling. Like someone snapping tiny elastic bands against her belly. Ash tries not to think about the little creatures burrowing into her. She focuses on the screen: a young couple arguing about their disastrous bathroom makeover.

For the first few days she forgets the *Hirudo adipolis* are inside her. Work is busy and the house is a disaster zone. She can't keep on top of it all. Dulcie makes 'potions' in the bath by squirting shampoo, conditioner and bodywash into old yoghurt containers, crumbling in bits of forgotten bath-bomb, slivers of ancient soap. Ash yells and Dulcie cries, says she wants Dad. Every surface of the bathroom is covered in potion slime. Ash shuts the door on it, makes macaroni cheese, lets Dulcie choose a Disney movie for them to watch together.

In the second week the *Hirudo adipolis* are on the move. Just a fluttering at first. Her belly is tighter, smaller. Her jeans are loose. When she finally gets around to cleaning the bathroom she can't hitch them up because of the rubber gloves. Dulcie sees her reaching up to clean the mirror and says, 'Mummy, your pants are falling down!' Ash doesn't let her pull them up. She doesn't want her to see the skin of her stomach up close. How it squirms and twitches.

After three weeks Ash's stomach is completely flat except for the rippling of the deposits. They wriggle from hip to hip, stretching her skin to their form like fingers under latex. They're more active at night. Sometimes Ash lies with her hand over them, just noticing the patterns they make. She can lie like that for hours, falling asleep with her hand there. She almost tells Sylvie about Ezy-Contour but decides not to.

All her old pants and skirts now fit her. Mel warned her about leaving the *Hirudo adipolis* in too long. Once they have extracted all the fat within a forty-centimetre radius they move into other parts of the body. It's important to take them out before that happens, so they don't go rogue. Ash has seen a picture of a woman who had one go up to her breast. It looked like she'd had a partial mastectomy.

But there's something about having them inside her. Ash doesn't think of them as deposits—that was just Ezy-Contour framing the language for their more squeamish customers. They're beings in their own right. Part of her, but separate too. Grown plump from her body. One of them is bigger than the others, darts around faster. Sometimes it loops around her navel like it's trying to get her attention. She pokes it, tells it to settle down.

To get them out you have to lay pieces of warm butter or streaky bacon on your belly and wait for the *Hirudo adipolis* to rupture the skin in search of the fresh fat. It's meant to happen quickly if they've consumed all the available local fat stores. Ash watches videos online of other people doing it. Usually someone helps with the removal clamp, stands close to the grease-covered skin, poised for the first eruptions. They pop out like plugs of sebum, fat and confident. But they really buck when the clamp grips them. They look like angry little legs, segmented rolls of fat kicking hopelessly.

Some of the extractions are filmed with a zoom lens and you can see their little blind eyes, their open mouths trying to suck fat from the air. The disposal boxes are lined with an acidic base and they stop moving as soon as they're dropped in. Sometimes the people on the videos laugh as they do this. It's a hysterical kind of laughter but it still seems callous. Ash got rid of her disposal box. She put it out with the rubbish after feeling the first loop around her belly button. She couldn't kill them like that.

The *Hirudo adipolis* thrash and twist against her waist now, forceful in their growing mass. Ash runs a bath when she is sure Dulcie is asleep. Then she puts half a block of butter in the microwave, watches it go round and round and pool in the bottom of the bowl. She takes it out, beats it with a wooden spoon until it's soft. In the bathroom, she puts the butter and the removal clamp on the vanity cabinet, takes off her clothes.

The bath is half filled so Ash's breasts, stomach and hips are above the water. She spreads the butter on with her hand, feels the little heads pushing up immediately. When the first one breaks through, she grabs it with the clamp and flicks it onto the tiled floor. It jerks around and then contracts itself like a caterpillar and tries to push itself forward on the slippery surface. It's as big as her pinky finger. The others squirm in the butter, mouths sucking. Ash flicks six more on the floor. Done.

She picks up the biggest one from the butter. It writhes in the clamp, startles her and she drops it in the bathwater. Panicked, she scoops it up in her palm and pinches it between the thumb and forefinger of her other hand to keep it from jumping off. It wriggles, tries to lunge forward. Tiny eyes blink. Ash pinches harder. The little 'o' of its mouth grows bigger. She squeezes, feels it give way.

The rupture tears open the mouth of the *Hirudo adipolis*. Ash's fat emerges from it in a gush. She holds the empty creature and the extruded fat up to her eyes. It's nothing now. Just dead skin and dead fat, which she wipes off her hand with a flannel. Then she gets the rest of them out of the butter and flicks them onto the floor. There are seventeen.

Ash wipes herself down with paper towels, blots the little wounds where the creatures came out. She has a shower to get rid of the grease, pumps out dollops of creamy bodywash until her palm is overflowing. The shape of her stomach is perfect now. She's so glad she did it. And Mel was right, it wasn't so bad removing them. She shouldn't have thrown away the disposal box, though. The *Hirudo adipolis* are squirming around on the tiles, mouths seeking. They might not die for ages.

Squeezing killed the big one—perhaps she could just squash them all. Ash fills her big stockpot with water and takes it into the bathroom with a roll of kitchen towels. She lays the kitchen towels over the writhing creatures, puts the pot on top to crush them.

Sitting on the toilet seat, Ash watches the water in the pot wobble then grow still. She thinks of people drowning kittens. Cries for a long time.

She needs to pull herself together; get it cleaned up before Dulcie wakes. Ash lifts the pot and scoops the mess up with kitchen towels, flushes it all down the toilet. Then she gets out some surface cleaner to spray the tiles—and notices one *Hirudo adipolis* still alive.

Dulcie is always rescuing snails, making them homes from takeaway containers, bringing them fresh grass and leaves. She would love to have a special new pet to care for. Ash finds an old pasta sauce jar and fills it with oil. Then she picks up the last *Hirudo adipolis* with the clamp and drops it in.

JORDAN HAMEL

Society does a collective impersonation of Robin Williams telling Matt Damon 'It's not your fault' repeatedly in *Good Will Hunting*

why do tsunamis have to be such try-hards   we get it you're wet
reject sincerity   as a mantra   a tonic   a life raft
reject melting pavements   don't leave *only footprints*   leave dick drawings
paint *hot enough for ya?*   on your neighbour's war machine

reject the sunrise   it's just the wildfires   the *Mean Girls* of the forest
take all the big yellow taxis   put em in a Counting Crows museum
never trust two sets of footprints in the sand   when they become one
carry only   what your chinchilla needs

curate your depression into different shades   of mood Frujus
made from dark web icecap chunks   tell everybody they're special
but not as special as you   tell everybody about the *old you*

orchestrate a small coup   to get on the coup ladder
kidnap Alanis Morissette   install her as the Minister for the Environment
exfoliate yourself   with basalt and sulphur   tell everyone
you're going natural   tell everyone   it wasn't you
it wasn't you   it couldn't have been you   tell everyone

imply it was them   don't they know there are microbeads in lube??
should've thought of that before they ...   now we're all fucked!   AMIRITE?!
test out your tight five at climate marches and memorial services

defund book clubs and karaoke   form craft circles instead
decorate each other's coffins   if you want to write messages of support
or encouragement   keep them on the underside of the lid

read your children privacy policies and heavy machinery manuals
make them debate the merits of data mining vs regular mining
give the winner a discounted mood Fruju   tell one person a day you love

the moment in a movie when a character says the name of the movie
tell one person a day   it wasn't you   tell them
until they believe you   tell them   until you believe yourself

only tell the sweat tunnel between your pillows   your fears
whisper the name of every person you've ever cared about
into the broken ceiling fan   then pray you outlive them all

ALISON GLENNY

from 'Small Plates'

1

My corona. Light circling luminous body, the moon is usual. Also an aureole, atmosphere's outermost layer. A faint halo or a natural consequence. Circular chandelier encourages daffodil trumpets, enamoured of leafy crowns, outgrowths. Charged conductors, cigars with blunt ends. Julieta smoking on her balcony scene is followed by a dirge or lamentation.

2

The poets move together in flocks. One finds a new song and the others take it up. Developers move in and the poets rise together to find a new perch. The night is a forest with missing eaves. So much wood taken to build boxes for poems to live in. Each leaf a quarrel over the exact placement of the moon.

LYNDSEY KNIGHT

serpent day

those little eels, the bootlaces, poking their heads up through the drainpipe that emptied into the river, just outside the coburns' place. one of their sons was yucky. a funny boy. a dirty bugger.

down the road, the walker boys watched their father work on the eel spears. the long wooden poles, rounded and smooth to hold, were once broom handles. he set four six-inch nails around the end of each pole. lashed them in place with strips of leather so the sharp ends of the nails pointed down. gave a good three inches to serve as a prong. with a hacksaw, he fashioned barbs.

while their father worked on the prongs, the boys watched wide-eyed and jiggling. when it took too long to stay polite, they strutted their anticipation around the back yard.

prong prong prong they said and collapsed into hysterical giggling. their father whistled as he worked; took his time, did a good job. do it once, do it right. he drilled a hole at the top of each broom handle, threaded a cord through, and fashioned loops to fit over small wrists. this way the spears could be fired from the bridge and not lost. spears that would last more than just a week or two. that was the story.

we'll get those bloody eels, the youngest said, as if the disruption they caused by living in the river was understood.

yeah. we'll prong 'em good and bring 'em home.

prong them with our prongs.

prong 'em through the back of the neck. ker-prong! KER-PRONG!

is that where you get them?

yeah, and you have to spear 'em hard. they're slippery. get away real fast if you don't do 'em hard and hold 'em down.

hold them down? I'm not touching the dirty buggers.

na, not touch. prong 'em and keep pushing down on the spear. hold 'em on the bottom of the river.

till the buggers die?

well, they go limp, anyway.

they set off like warriors, eel spears in their right hands, caps pulled low over their eyes. the tin bucket bumping against the older one's skinny leg, empty and full of hollow ringing. they passed the drainpipe at the coburns' place, checked for bootlaces, and crossed the road to the footbridge. on the other side of the river the grass was long, up to your waist even. the riverbank on that side was rough and seemed far away. flax bushes and long grass gave you that māori feeling.

at the middle of the footbridge they stopped and looked down. the river was clear and moved steadily beneath them. when they were little, they had leaned over the side of the footbridge with their mother to feed bread to the ducks. and to the eels. they had been too small to reach their arms over the wooden rail, so they had climbed up the wire sides and stood with sandalled feet poking through.

it's a good flow here for pooh sticks, the smaller boy remembered. his brother didn't answer. he was watching the coburn boy who always seemed to be where they were. he was there now, crossing the road, heading for the bridge.

what do ya reckon eels have inside them?

eel flesh. and guts.

what's their guts look like? the yucky guy had turned back from crossing the bridge at the call of his mother.

gooky of course. plenty of gook. and water. living in the river they swallow a lot of water. there'll be poo too. a fair bit of poo, I reckon.

they looked down at the river some more. little silveries flashed in and out of the river weed and darted upstream, six inches of flickering light. and then, there were the eels! three dark shapes gliding between the shadows of the willows, slipping along sideways, roping their shadowy way upstream. fins up by their faces, white underbellies flashing.

prong them, come on! prong them now! yelled the older one. his spear shot down into the water with the force of someone much older. get them! the smaller boy let his spear fly down beside his brother's.

it doesn't matter. they deserve it. the dirty buggers.

CADENCE CHUNG

that's why they call me missus fahrenheit

oh, gals, I'm at   440Hza
    doing my makeup in the McDonald's bathroom
leaving glitter trails in the sink   lipstick-covered
    toilet paper smudging its way down   the faucet
honey, i'm going a mile a minute   humming along
    to the invisible choir   in the pulpit
and by invisible choir   i mean any tacky Arcade Fire song
    playing through shop speakers
that stinks of teen angst and Doc Martens   covered
    in signatures and scribbles.   babe, i'm going crazy
all alone with that flirting moon   dripping
    in the sky   smoking it out yellow   through
my window   never deciding on her look
    but always with a cut-crease   and endless
sweeps of silver highlighter.   sweetie, if i were
around in Byron's time   you bet i'd go wild
    writing endless sappy sonnets   about trees
if i compared a tree to my mind i bet they'd all go
    absolutely apeshit   i saw a mushroom today
in my back yard   bet i could write about its soft
silver gills, its spores springing   to my finger's
    warm touch.   girl, i'm so mad i'm getting tender
about a mushroom   i'm getting tender about
    everything   because everything's too bitter
to not suck on the sweet bits   making every lick last
    like a lolly on a car trip   an eyeshadow
from a discontinued line.   oh gals, i'm up for
    burning myself electric   calling out
every compliment i can think of   for every pair

of pretty earrings there's a pretty girl, another
    way i can squeeze my skin   into someone else's
life, linger there   for longer than my due. baby,
i'm reading Shakespeare on the bus   next to a man
    who's blowing gently   on his harmonica
and i think i understand   why my mother
    always took too long to grab her coat   always
stayed for another coffee   because when you're
    wild with love you always want
someone else to share it with.   girlie,
i'm trying to barrel into every person   i come across
    and by barrel, i mean smile, and by smile
i mean stay   i'm going crazy trying to live
    trying to cover myself in glitter   to hide the dust
but gals, i like it   i like walking out of McDonald's
with pink eyeshadow on   that definitely
    wasn't there before. you know, nobody
even notices   if you look like you know
    what you're doing   maybe if i look like
i'm doing things wildly   patching together
    every scrap and semblance i know of, like
a mismatched outfit   of love   then someone
    will stop me   slow me down   tell me
that they like my earrings   ask me
    where i got them from

BRENT KININMONT

Crossed Toes

What effect a mermaid's union with a human might have on the descendants is unknown.

They're genetic, the sports doctor says.
Not, as you'd expect, from a childhood packing

extra-wide feet into regular shoes,
like batter into madeleine moulds.

For a second opinion I would need the ocean
and a bench looking over it.

My birth mother would wear sandals (as would I),
and when it felt less like a blind date—

having never met really,
she would uncoil her legs (long, like mine).

Behind my ocean gaze, I would scan for
the smallest toes nestled on their sides,

and for that fourth toe tucked under a third where
the skin on long hikes always blisters.

Then this daydreaming might end.
About lopping off the crooked digits,

and with the others pointing in
the direction I am running,

the invaluable seconds
I could trim from my times.

REBECCA STYLES

Limpet

'I've forgotten the name for these.' I rub my hand along a small hard white shell that's clinging to a rock. I look up at Conrad. Even though he's off duty—he works for Fisheries New Zealand—he's keeping an eye on the divers to make sure they are out of the marine reserve.

'A limpet. It hangs on to the rock and moves to feed at high tide. After feeding it'll return to the same spot.'

'The exact same spot?'

Conrad squats down to get a closer look, his knees up to his chin, and gently brushes his index finger around the indentations of the shell. 'Yeah, they leave behind a trail like a snail does, and they have this foot that helps them stick. Eventually they start looking like the rock.'

The colour of the rocks reminds me of when I spilt a test pot of paint on the lean-to at the back door. I must have been seven or eight. I had been poking at a paint tin with a piece of splintered kindling, wanting to open the tin but knowing I would be in trouble if I did. A nagging compulsion to open it, open it, took over and I put the edge of the kindling under the lid's lip and the paint spilt onto the piece of wood, my fingers and the concrete slab floor. I can still see the thick brown paint sliding down the lean-to's rough-edged timber framing. I knew I needed to do something about it. I called out. My stepdad Frank came, breath malty with beer, picked up the tin, grabbed my wrist and pulled me to the tub beside the washing machine where he roughly wiped my hands with muttoncloth doused with turps. The smell stung like a slap. I cried while he told me off.

The divers' black-skinned bodies slip beneath the surface.

Conrad collects seaweed outside the reserve. 'It's wakame, a Japanese native but it grows well here. I add it to food.'

'Like salt?'

'Like salt. Good in miso soup.'

Sometimes he brings his daughter along when we go for walks on the beach. Brianna likes to point out the jellyfish that are the same lurid pink as dishwashing liquid; she picks them up, runs at me, shakes the jellyfish, I stand back in mock fright, and then she throws the jellyfish back down on the beach.

The first time I met Brianna we played with plasticine in Conrad's lounge. We had gone to the playground but it started raining as soon as Brianna had climbed to the top of the jungle gym in her jandals, so we went home and ate egg sandwiches and the butterfly cupcakes I had made to impress her. I had scooped out the middle of each cupcake, cut the removed conical piece of cake in half, filled in the hole with cream, and poked the cut pieces, like wings, carefully into the cream, sprinkling them with raspberry jelly crystals.

Brianna ate two of the cupcakes while we sat at the coffee table rolling plasticine into worms, and curling worms into snails.

Frank turns seventy next week. I'm flying down south for the party. He didn't want any fuss so it'll just be me, my sister Kate, her husband, and Mum. She has ordered a cake from Pak'nSave. A picture of Frank will be iced onto it.

'What picture is it?' I asked Mum on the phone.

'A hunting one. A picture of him with a gun and a couple of dead ducks in his hand. Your sister found it.'

'Does he want anything for his birthday?'

'No, he doesn't need anything.'

Once, on a family holiday, Kate and I built a snowman in front of the caravan. I had run in to tell Mum and Frank about it—I wanted them to come out and see—but I slipped and smacked my chin on the caravan floor, which made Frank fly off the handle.

The louvre windows in Conrad's bedroom are open but the curtains are drawn, even though it's the middle of the day. The curtains get sucked against the window and then blown out again. He's always a little coy when we sleep together during the day; he pulls the blinds even though no one is likely to look in the bedroom window from the yard. Sometimes I would just like to lie on the bed and feel the sunshine on my skin, softening, flowing.

Before we went to bed, Conrad washed the seaweed in the kitchen sink and draped it on the plastic clothes-horse in the spare room. The smell is already starting to permeate the house.

It was the third or fourth time I stayed over that he showed me Brianna's bedroom. Before that I had cast furtive glances into the room but couldn't see anything beyond the blue of the walls and curtains, and the bedclothes bunched at the end of the bed.

'Come and see this,' he said. 'Brianna's made a house out of boxes for her Barbie.'

Brianna had positioned Barbie in the corner of a cardboard lounge. Beside Barbie was a coffee table made out of white photocopy paper that she had coloured in with a purple glitter pen. She had pushed a knitting needle along the length of the box and draped Barbie's pink and purple jacket and glitter-starred trousers on it.

I wonder if Barbie is still sitting in her cardboard lounge. I can't remember Frank taking any interest in anything that I played with. I put my hand up to Conrad's face and brush my fingers against the whiskers he doesn't bother shaving when he's off duty.

'You're a good dad.'

He opens his eyes, pulls me closer and kisses me on the forehead.

'Frank hardly took us out anywhere. You're always out and about with Brianna, and letting her have friends over. It's great that she's become interested in the sea—jellyfish and so on.'

Conrad smiles. When he runs his hand through my hair I can feel how sea salt has thickened the strands.

'Frank took us to the rock pools once,' I say. 'Behind the freezing works. I lost my balance walking on the rocks and fell. I managed to graze my arm from my wrist to my elbow.' I rub my arm as I explain—it feels cold and smooth where it once bubbled with blood.

'Frank told me to put my arm in the seawater because the salt would take the pain away.'

I hadn't cried, even though Frank had said, 'For God's sake, girl, stick your arm in the water.'

While my skin absorbed the sting of sea salt and Frank's words, I stared at a white oval shell stuck to a rock and wondered how hard it was.

The next day, Brianna opens the oven door and the sponge drops in its tin.

'No, don't do that! You'll ruin it!'

The oven door slams shut as Brianna lets go and runs to her room, tears already falling.

I bring my hands up to my face, close my eyes. Shit. I can't believe I snapped, snapped the way Frank snapped.

Brianna had wanted to make a huge butterfly cake. I explained before we started that I'd never made a huge one before but reckoned if we made a sponge in a round cake tin it would be the same thing. Brianna wants it to look like a monarch butterfly because she has a swan plant at her mum's house and has been watching the butterflies emerge from their chrysalises, so I bought orange jelly crystals and some black jellybeans to decorate the cake with.

I stare up the hallway that leads to Brianna's bedroom, past the clothes dryer and washing machine at the back door, above which is a white shelf with shells that Brianna and her dad have collected on their beach walks. I rub my arm where I grazed it all those years ago.

It should be easy enough to say sorry, though I'm not sure how these apologies sound. After an incident with Frank had run its course it was like he wiped it from his mind, and when he sobered up he didn't understand why we were giving him a wide berth. I can remember watching his genuine puzzlement, his eyes wounded and thin lips downcast, whenever we ignored or avoided him.

I walk towards Brianna's room.

As I pass the shelf, I see a limpet shell. Its underside shines like it's captured some sun.

BRIDGET REWETI
NGĀTI RANGINUI, NGĀI TE RANGI

Known Seas

TBC#1, 2021, stereoscopic C-Type photograph
TBC#2, 2021, stereoscopic C-Type photograph
TBC#3, 2021, stereoscopic C-Type photograph
TBC#4, 2021, stereoscopic C-Type photograph
TAU#1, 2021, stereoscopic hand-coloured photograph
TAU#2, 2021, stereoscopic hand-coloured photograph
TAU#3, 2021, stereoscopic hand-coloured photograph
TAU#4, 2021, stereoscopic hand-coloured photograph

This series of stereoscopic photographs shows Te Tai-o-Ārai-te-uru around Otepōti and the base of Mauao in Tauranga Moana. Inverting Allen Curnow's poem 'Landfall in Unknown Seas', I've chosen to show the seas and the lands they surround as known, named and so implicitly possessing long-held narratives pre-dating 1642.

Stereoscopic photographs create a three-dimensional image when viewed through a stereoscope. Their duality combines to form the perception of a deeper space. 'Free viewing' is a term that describes seeing a stereoscopic image in 3-D without a stereoscope: if you hold the page at the right distance, and focus as if looking through the image towards a horizon, the sense of space will appear. This blurring and refocusing is similar to 'Magic Eye' optical illusions.—Bridget Reweti

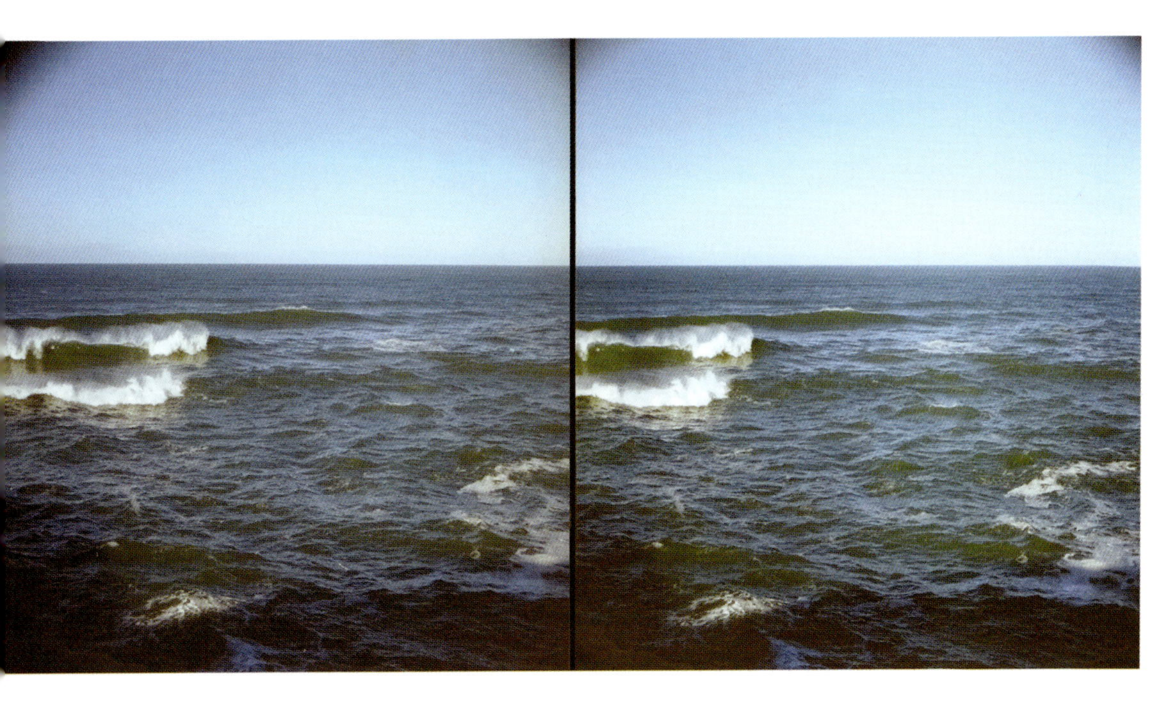

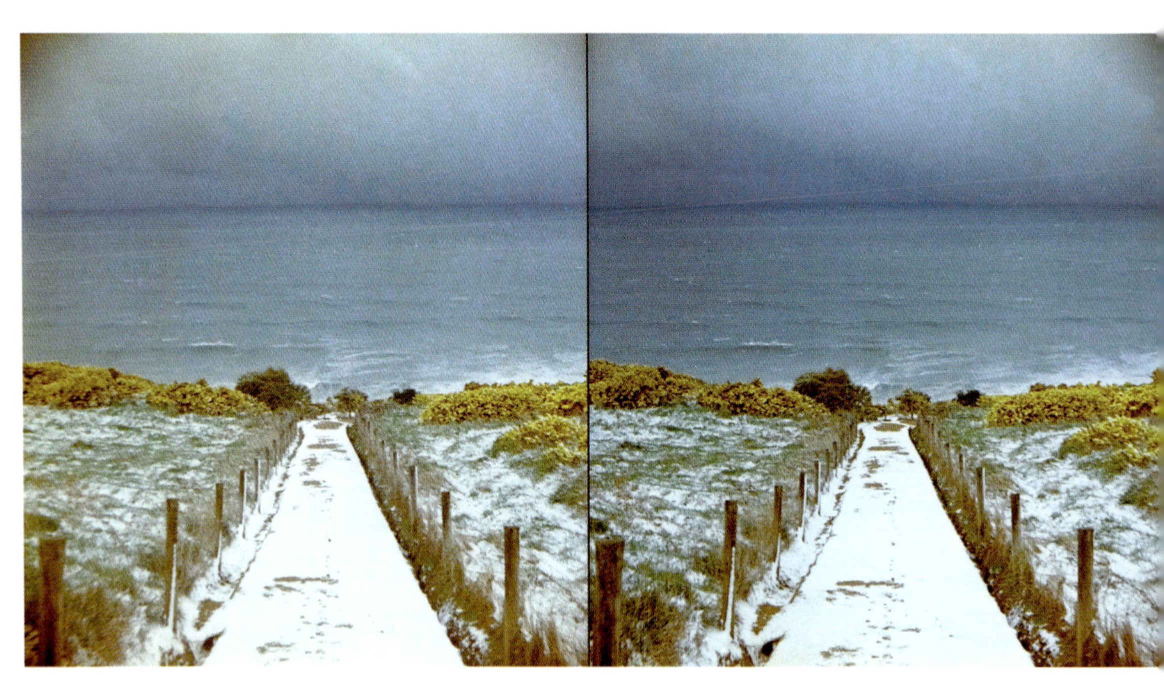

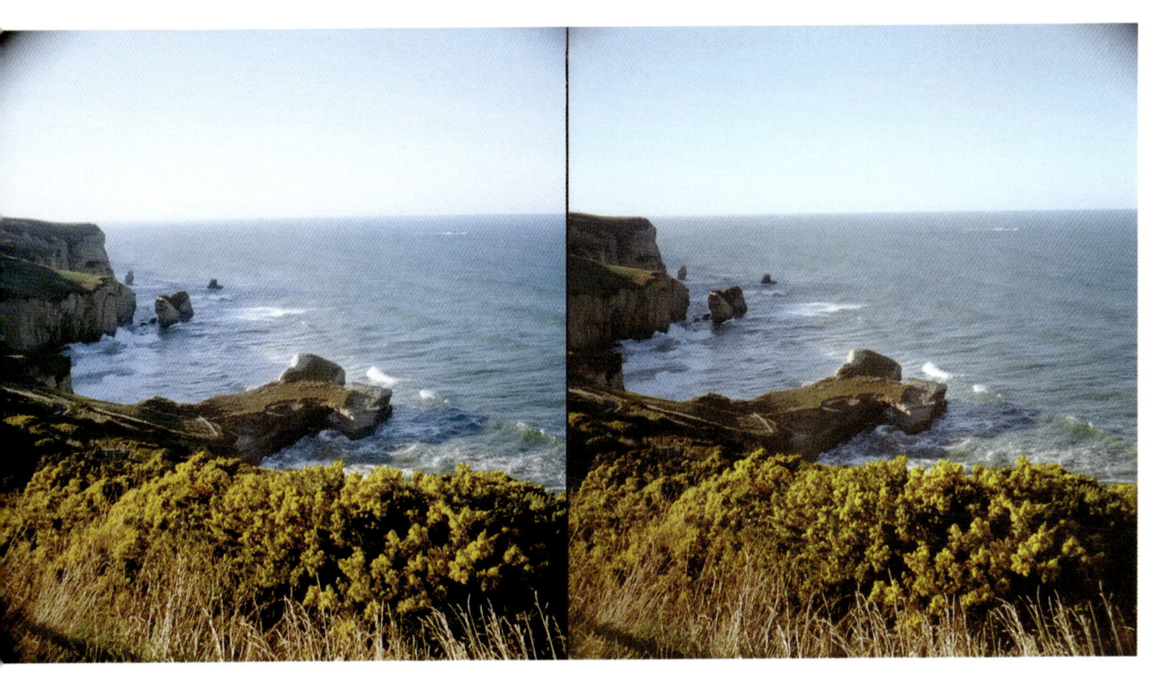

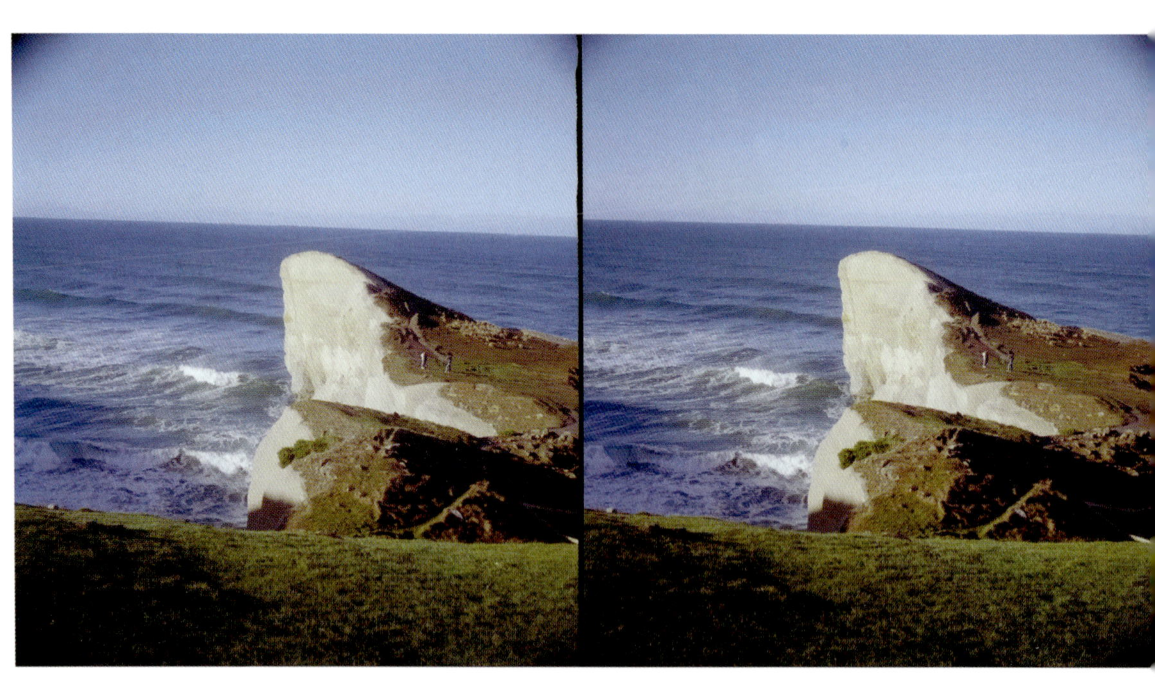

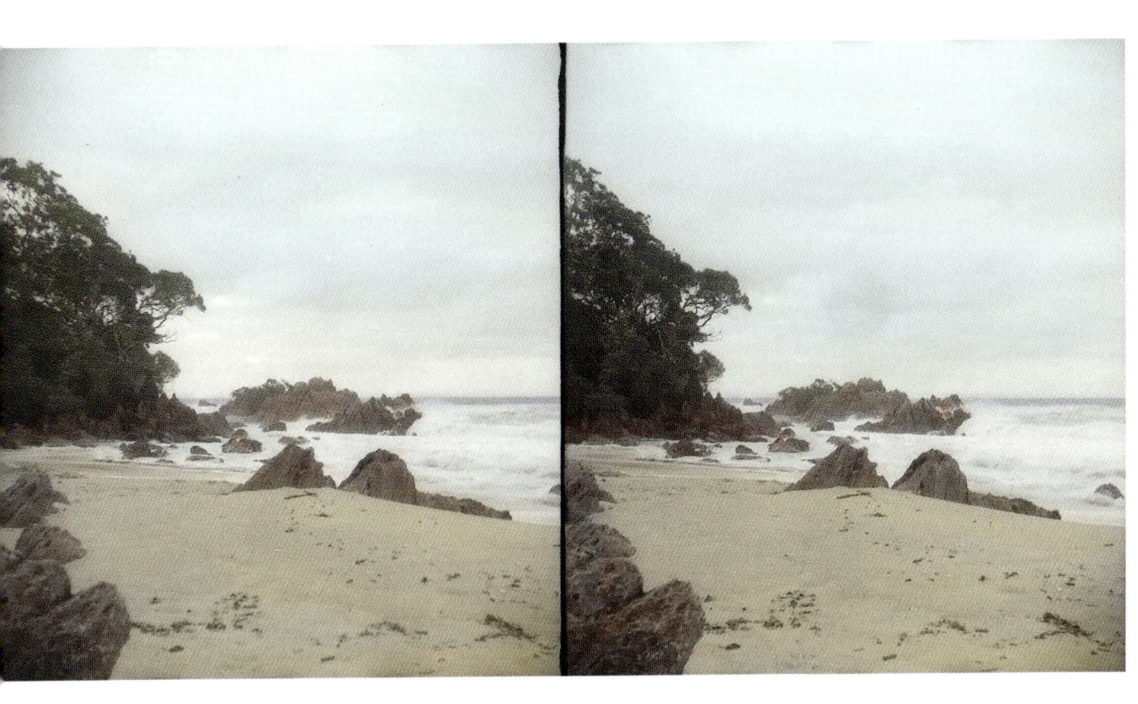

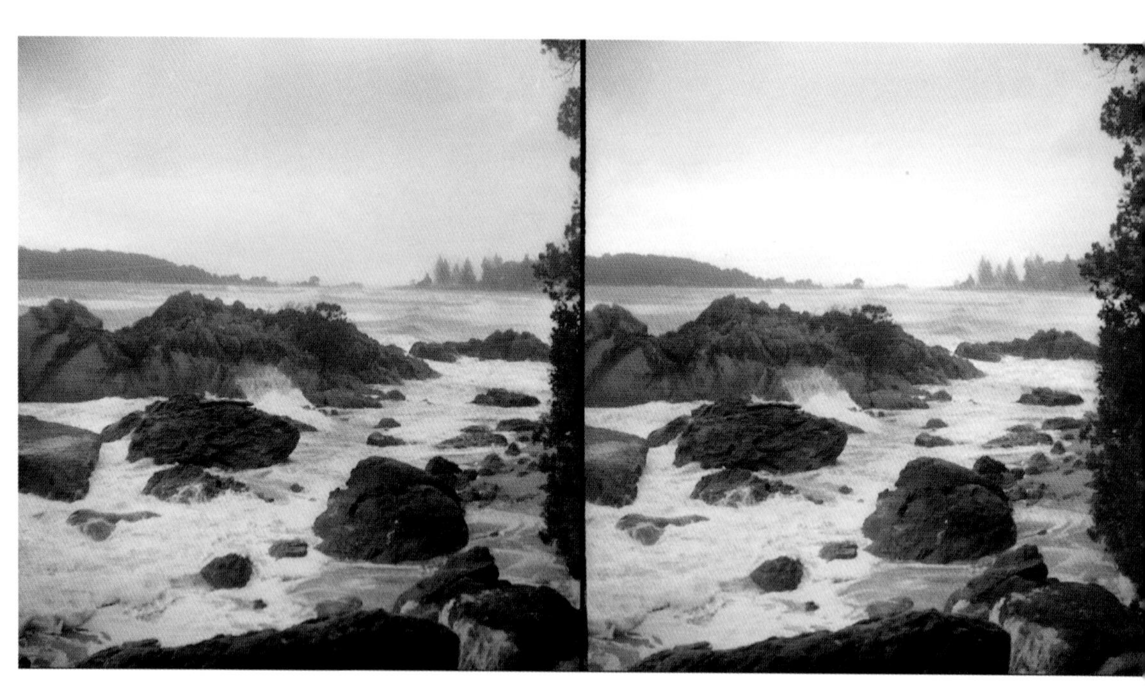

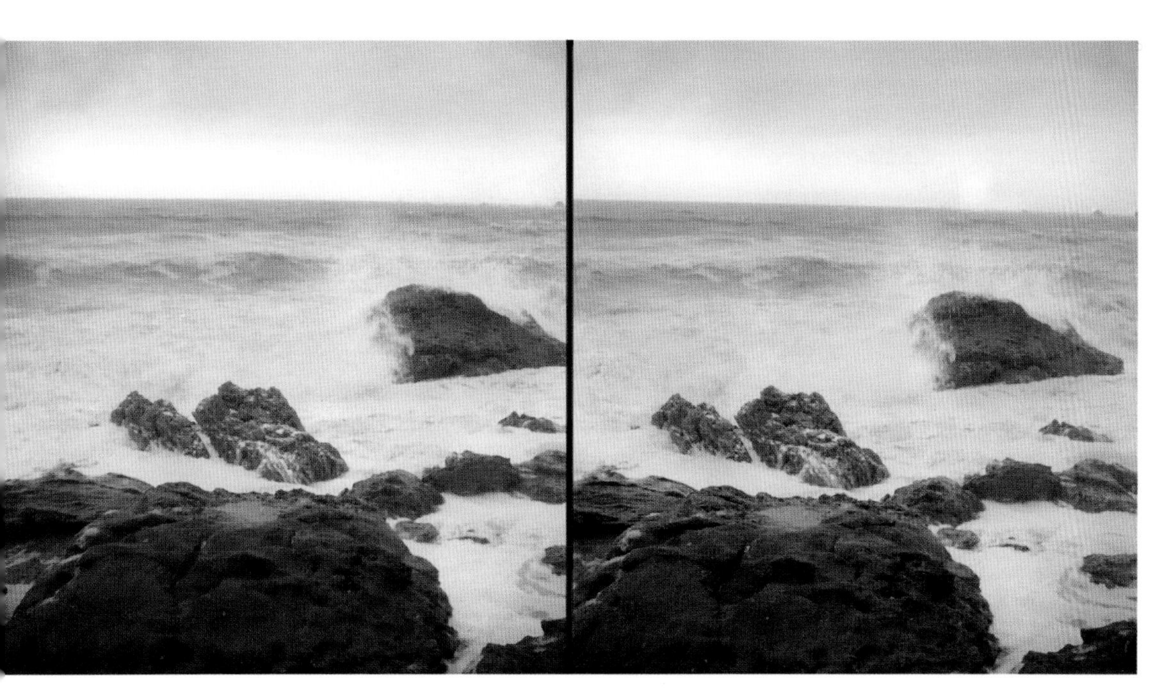

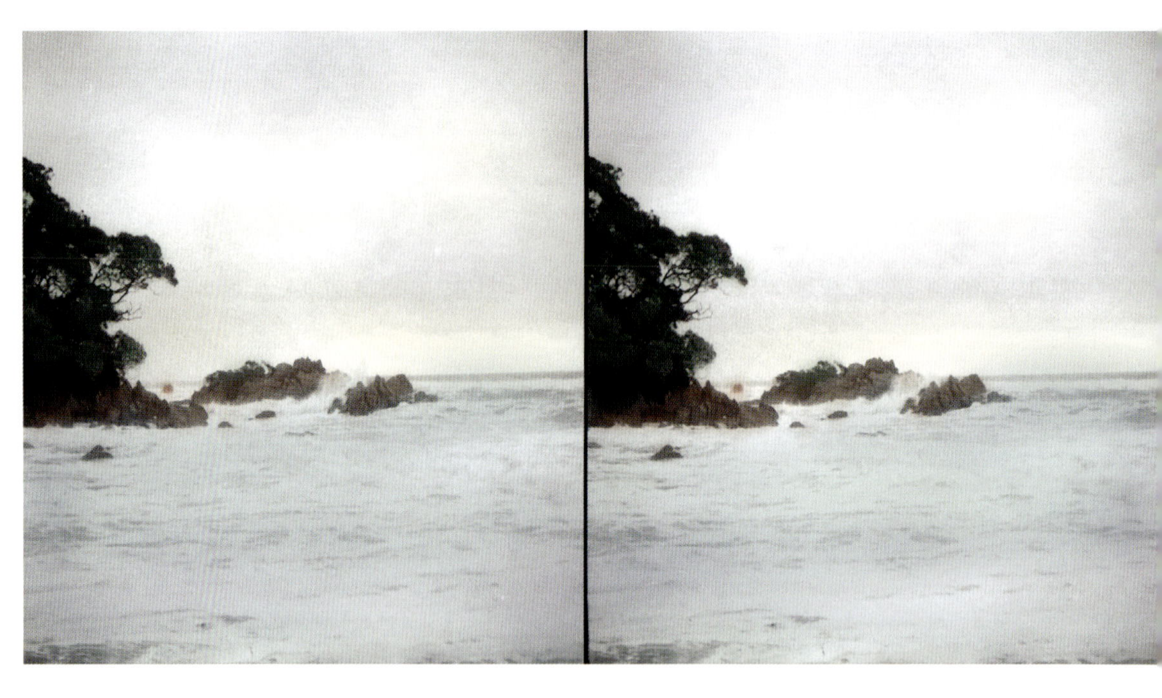

KIRSTY BAKER

Leaf, Foreshore, Seed

To produce her exhibition *And we look and comb our hair*, Bekah Carran cast a series of everyday objects as sculptural forms, bestowing them with an elusive significance. A single branch pierces the base of a spherical pot, tilting it off balance, while also supporting its precariously balanced weight. The branch curves through and out of the pot, arcing through the air above it, anchored low by a single suspended cup. Elsewhere, clusters of bowls are pushed up against one another, filled with a range of inconsequential objects: a tiny spoon, a solitary earring forever lost to its partner, something that looks like a walnut. By casting these objects and presenting them to us as inexplicable offerings, Carran grants permanence to the detritus that we can't quite bring ourselves to cast from our lives. As I inspect a jumble of vessels contained within vessels, I wonder how these objects may once have been connected to people.

I think, too, of a collection of objects that my partner and I have kept. Neither used nor discarded, they lie nestled in the bottom of our son's chest of drawers. A hospital bracelet, a set of tiny heart monitoring pads, a mechanism that once linked his newborn body to the C-PAP machine that helped him to breathe. Now they lie useless—or, more accurately, lacking in purpose. They were thrust into our hands as keepsakes by a nurse upon discharge; we had no idea what to do with them. Abandoned to the chaos of the bottom drawer, they have become strangely talismanic, pointing insistently to what might have been.

Two days after our baby was born I read a news report about an investigation into two cases of insufficient foetal monitoring at a nearby hospital. In each instance the labours described echoed my own almost exactly: a string of medical events that occur frequently enough to be considered commonplace. An overdue baby results in an induced labour. Significant foetal distress necessitates an emergency caesarean. And yet the experience of living through these events feels anything but normal. After he is born, our son is rushed immediately to Neonatal Intensive Care, where he spends the first week of his life. In the wake of his violent departure from my body, he seems utterly extraordinary. One of the babies I read about did not survive, while the other was left with significant brain damage. Our son, so astonishing already, is rendered strangely miraculous in light of this news. The line that delineates the everyday and the tragic is stretched thin, a fine meniscus, prone to rupture at any moment as a result of the smallest of decisions. The decision to monitor one baby. The decision not to monitor another. One lives. One dies. Our son's wildly erratic heart rate is detected. He lives.

Each night the stagnant air in the too-hot maternity ward is punctuated by the sounds of sharp, insistent cries from other rooms. The deep ache of my child's absence settles on me heavily, pulled taut each time a baby demands maternal comfort. I think of our son, warmed and monitored in his plastic box, and sob gently. I think too of the mothers who were not so lucky and know that, in general, my good fortune is not a simple matter of luck. It is a result of privilege.

In Aotearoa the devastating impact of colonisation continues to assert itself, even in childbirth. Generations of entrenched systemic racism have resulted in poor maternal health, and neonatal mortality rates that are disproportionately high among Māori and Pasifika. When a nurse asks my son's ethnicity for one of countless forms, I reply that he's Tangata Tiriti, but she can put Pākehā. 'There's no box for that,' she says. 'I'll put New Zealand European.' In another room my son's obsessively monitored heart continues to beat, his lungs continue their assisted inflation and deflation. I gather my luck and privilege around me like a protective cloak that I did nothing to earn, and hope for sleep.

My hospital room has a large window that looks across a flat concrete roof onto another wing of the hospital, rising up to block out any hints of the natural world. The window, inevitably, cannot be opened. The air inside the room hangs heavy with artificial heat and sterility. The week I spend in here feels like a claustrophobic eternity. I'm unsurprised by how untethered the lack of fresh air makes me feel. I grow increasingly desperate to smell the salt tang of the wind, to hear the pulse of the ocean, or to walk in the loamy bush after a heavy rain. My sense of place and belonging has always been deeply rooted in the natural world, in the slow connection you build with a place whose hills and coasts you've walked and re-walked many times. I've imagined my footsteps stitching me to the fabric of this country, this home that I have chosen after visiting from Scotland fifteen years ago. I'm aware, too, that the colonial framework within which I was raised and educated taught me to see my relationship to the land this way: as if occupation is belonging, familiarity is ownership.

There is an image saved on my phone, a photograph taken in the darkened hum of the Adam Art Gallery Te Pātaka Toi in 2018, to which I return again and again in that hospital room. The image shows a triptych of brightly framed photographs, unevenly spaced and of slightly differing dimensions. The photographs, made by Ngahuia Harrison as part of her work *Ngā Paepae Tapu*, offer a series of objects suspended in a state of in between: seeds before they germinate; leaves detached from the tree that gave them life but not yet shrivelled; the intertidal zone that is at once land and ocean, solid ground made liquid. The images depict thresholds burdened with possibilities, fragments of the natural world laden with life.

The seed, a heart. The leaf, a lung. The water of the foreshore, the life-blood.

Looking at the photograph I have taken, I think at first that I'm looking at kawakawa leaves, though their shape and the pink flowerbuds on the edge of the picture prove me wrong. Nonetheless, I'm reminded of the leaves picked to place on the office door of a dear friend upon his death. I was pregnant at his funeral, but newly so. Early enough that the strange comfort I felt at this new life beginning to unfurl was unknown to those sitting beside me. My child, growing within me like a secret, felt as though it meant something. It felt as though this potential new life suddenly mattered more, as we gathered collectively to say goodbye to one so loved. The collective love for one lost was strangely reassuring. Sitting through the funeral service I felt calmed by a belief that this love would find a way into the new heart pulsing within me.

Now the secret has been made physical, the abstract rendered viscerally, messily real. Enclosed in sterile plastic, my baby's temperature and breathing are regulated, his heart monitored. Persistent bleeps and frequent alarms shape the aural pattern of his existence. No birds sing here, there is no breeze to carry the smell of the earth or the tang of the ocean. I want to bring the world to him: to lay great, lush, heaping strands of leaves around him. I imagine the leaves of the kawakawa and the kōwhai, laid down beside those of the rowan and the hazel. I imagine their rich chlorophyll green oxygenating the air. I imagine they hold the power to consume the heavy air, to absorb the fear and pain of those who keep vigil in these wards, the oxygen they expel filling the tiny pathways of my son's damaged lungs.

The intertidal water of Harrison's photograph provokes a yearning for the ocean familiar to those of us born and raised on islands, but my emotive response pushes me up against the limits of my belonging in this country. The European lens through which I have been taught to see the leaf, the foreshore and the seed is a persistent discomfort. I think it is this—their ability to remind me of the limits of my cultural understanding, their insistent reminder that connection comes with obligation—that has lodged Harrison's photographs so firmly in my consciousness.

For the Atlantic is not the Pacific. I do not belong to the waters that pulse each day over the fringes of this land. The circumference of my childhood can instead be measured in wind-abraded basalt shores, in stepped volcanic slopes plunging into the chill of oceanic waters unimaginably far from here. Our son's childhood, however, will be contained by the swell and thrum of Pacific waters. He will learn to walk, to stumble and run over *this* earth. It is our obligation to teach him that his familiarity is not ownership, that his occupation of this land offers a specific kind of belonging.

Whenua / land; whenua / placenta.

To be of this land is to be birthed by it, by the blood of connectivity tying placenta to earth to ocean to people. I can learn these words, but this is not my language and this is not my earth. I am the descendant of the thieves of language, the violators of land. Our son, like us, is here not by virtue of that earth, but by virtue of a treaty. A treaty both mistranslated and repeatedly contravened by the Crown. The earth upon which he will walk was taken from Māori by his European ancestors. It was stolen by force and deception, claimed through bloodshed and the manipulation of both law and language. These are the wreaths of history that I must lay at my son's feet. This is the sprawling mesh of land and ocean into which he has been born, and into which he will walk, step by tentative step.

But for now, as he lies in his incubator, propped on his front to help his tiny lungs inflate, I imagine instead wreaths of kōwhai and rowan, strands of kawakawa and hazel.

ETHAN TE ORA

Paper Crowns, Bucket Hats

I am the man, I suffered, I was there—Walt Whitman

I walked head down through high school until Raj Singh transferred from Tauranga Boys'. It made me feel giddy to win the friendship of someone so funny. Back then, I assumed that everyone must love him. Now I realise I was one of the few who did.

His face alone was a perfect act of rebellion. At a school where the powers that be judged morality according to smoothness of skin, he escaped censure over immaculate three-day stubble.

It was true that I heard him say offensive things to almost everyone at one time or another. He was charismatic and able to get away with such things. He would just talk about how he hated everyone equally, which excused any behaviour in those days. I didn't really say much of anything, offensive or otherwise, to anyone. Nor did I stand up for myself when offensive things were said about me. Unless Raj was the person saying them. I eventually developed mechanisms to cope.

There was nothing unusual about any of this. That was life at an all-boys' school. I sometimes think about those experiences: the complicated ways they damaged us, and must continue to harm people we come into contact with. But I don't dwell on those thoughts for long.

Raj appeared like a rainbow on my emotional landscape and for a while the clouds seemed to clear. For one thing, he negotiated our schedules in ways that meant most of our seventh-form year was spent not in a classroom. He somehow convinced teachers in four out of six subjects that we were studying towards Scholarship exams, and the best environment for this would be unsupervised at the school library. I don't even know how he did it, and I would've been standing right there when he did.

Those rare study periods when we actually went to the library were spent honing Raj's standup routine. I don't remember any of the jokes today, which should tell you everything. But at the time I thought he was hilarious. Raj loved Eddie Murphy's first two standup specials and Chris Rock's later ones. Eventually one of us discovered Richard Pryor, who we both came to love most and whose material has aged much better. We were in the habit of spontaneously acting out different bits from Eddie Murphy's *Delirious*, or Richard Pryor's *Live in Concert*, in everyday conversation.

The two of us even saw Chris Rock perform at the Civic in 2008. I remember Rock was in the process of telling a joke, using Aids as a punchline, when a stage light exploded behind him. The comedian froze, then said a certain group of people must be mad at him. Except he used a homophobic term that I won't give power by repeating here. The point is that Raj laughed so hard the paper crown slipped from his head. Earlier that night we had eaten at Burger King, and the crowns came folded into the bag with our meals. Raj insisted we both wear them, calling himself the Burger Mahārāja. I 'misplaced' mine in the restroom before we left, but he wore his the rest of the night and the whole trip back to Hamilton. I even remember seeing the crumpled crown displayed proudly on his bedside dresser a few months later, which is a little bit sad when you think about it.

Most study periods we didn't go to the library, instead going to KFC. On one such occasion we were walking down Grey Street when we passed a Thai restaurant.

'Do Christina's parents own that restaurant?' he asked me.

'Chris is Cambodian.'

'True, bro, true.'

'Not everyone's parents can own a dairy in Putaruru.'

'Fuck off,' he said. 'It's a superette, mate.'

We stopped at the lights.

'Christina is feral,' he said. 'She needs a haircut.'

Christina was my girlfriend of two years, who hadn't cut her hair in six years, owing to some deeply entrenched view she would not be attractive without ringlets reaching down to her waist. I adored her hair. It smelled intoxicatingly of cocoa butter, applied to define the curls, and became like a second pillow when I spooned her after sex.

'Chris isn't feral.'

'Remind me again how to say dick in *Cambodian*?' He had intentionally placed the emphasis of that sentence on the last word to annoy me.

'The *Khmer* for penis is ling.'

'Ding-a-ling-ling!' he said and dribbled an empty Coke can like a football as we crossed the road.

I decided to bait him. 'What's the word for female dog in Indian?'

'Bro, how many times do I have to tell you: Indian isn't a language. It's Hindi. And it's kutti, you fucking kutti.' Obviously, I knew this. He was always speaking in Hindi to friends on his Nokia 3310, berating them with a chorus of kuttis.

'Saei kadaoy,' I said, which was one of the few other Khmer phrases Christina had taught me. It meant *whatever*. I pronounced the word exactly as she did, putting on an exaggerated Valspeak accent like Cher Horowitz from *Clueless*.

We navigated congested midday traffic, crossing the road to our promised land.

'It's weird when you try to put expression in your voice,' he said, 'because all I hear is *error, error, I am a robot*.' I had a deeper voice than practically anyone else our age, and this was a wellspring of amusement for him. He stopped then, in the middle of the busy road, and performed a series of stiff-arm movements, meant to match the robotic monotone. The only way to shut down such taunts was to join in. I started to mimic his arm motions and then froze, pretending I had malfunctioned.

'Stupid fucking Bitch Fingers,' he said, laughing.

Bitch Fingers was a nickname he had given me on account of Mrs Redpath, our sixth-form English teacher, who remarked that I had long, graceful fingers, like a pianist. At first I protested, meaning of course the nickname stuck.

I pushed open the door to KFC and there she was again. Not Mrs Redpath. A woman behind the counter to whom I was related. I didn't know exactly how we were related, but we were. Raj, who was preternaturally obsessed with caste, always found the fact of her working there delicious. She must be at least sixty-five, judging from the deep smile wrinkles, and her shock of white hair beneath a navy KFC cap.

'Kia ora, Aunty,' I said. 'How are you?'

'Aww, kia ora, boy!' She gave me the sunniest high-beam smile. She always looked so happy to be there. KFC should have put her on a billboard. 'Heard your dad's in a wheelchair now. Diabetes, eh? Same sad story.'

'My dad's not in a wheelchair, Aunty. I'm Lee's son.'

'Sorry, boy! Always getting my mokos confused.' She gave me the loveliest smile then, somehow lovelier than the first one. It was a smile that transmitted a flowing sense of aroha, but more specifically told me *sorry about the confusion, I will give you only thigh pieces in your bucket*. It really warmed my heart to see it.

'Staff discount, Aunty?' I said, which was a little joke we shared.

'Oh, you!'

I turned away from the counter feeling strong affection towards her, and at the same time embarrassment at having seen her there again. It was a confusing headspace to occupy. I walked over to the table where Raj now sat, leaning forward eagerly. He had ordered from the other counter and already had his bucket. The two of us observed a certain rule of etiquette, otherwise uncommon among us, where neither one broke a wing before the other.

'Have you noticed,' he said, 'that you only speak Māori around Māoris?'

'You only speak Hindi when you speak to other Indians.'

'But I actually speak the language,' he said. 'You've got like two phrases you trot out. And you only do it around KFC Lady and Mrs Barton.'

Mrs Barton was the Māori Studies teacher. She made kids sing waiata in front of the whole class if they were even just a few minutes late. The one time I was late she gave me an assertive nod and told me to take a seat. The whole class protested but she must have known making me sing would be too cruel. We are related as well. *Kia ora, Whaea Barton.*

'I never noticed I did that.'

He toyed restlessly with a wing in his bucket. 'You're from the tribe that owns everything, eh?'

I knew that he meant Tainui. He always spoke disparagingly about them. Tainui had land returned as part of a landmark Treaty of Waitangi settlement around ten years ago, including important Hamilton sites where Waikato Hospital and Waikato University stood. Tainui had built a monolithic shopping complex, known as Te Awa, The Base. Now The Base had Hamilton's CBD in a death grip, drawing away retail customers in droves. Some people hated Tainui for this reason.

'I'm Ngāti Maniapoto. The one with the warriors.'

'That's right,' he said. 'The *dumb* warriors.'

Raj was loosely referencing my history project about the Battle of Ōrākau, known as Rewi's last stand. The battle occurred at a pivotal moment during the Invasion of Waikato, in 1864. Rewi Maniapoto and his warriors had found themselves outnumbered and surrounded on all sides by colonial forces. The pā was cut off from any water supply. The noose tightened; the bloodbath just a matter of time. But Rewi led a daring escape in the night, avoiding a total massacre. Raj was showing that he remembered, in other words showing that he cared.

'Exactly,' I said.

My order was called and I walked to the counter, sidestepping a small puddle of Pepsi on my way. KFC seemed to be doing a roaring trade that afternoon. There were several others who had brazenly wagged in full school uniform. I picked up my bucket from the counter, stealing glances at the greasy bounty on my way back to the table. It was just as I suspected: nothing but thighs.

Raj peered over. 'Score—all thighs!' Then he gripped my upper thigh.

The two of us ate ravenously.

'So, bro,' he said with a full mouth, 'are you gonna apply for one of the Māori grants at uni?'

'Nah, I'm not Māori enough.'

I knew you needed just one great-grandparent who was Māori to qualify for scholarships. But I still felt I wasn't Māori *enough*. As in, I was fair-skinned and didn't have the reo.

'Are you sure? You should check.'

'I'm pretty sure.'

I should mention that Raj had used *uni* as a generic, but it wouldn't take us long to get there.

'I still don't get why you're going to Wintec.'

There it was.

'Let's not do this again.'

'But you're smarter than me, and I'm smarter than everyone.' He wiped his greasy mouth with his jersey. 'I just don't get it.'

Raj had applied to study law at Auckland University. I planned to complete a BMA of journalism at Wintec—a technical institution.

'You're gonna end up like Happy Pills over there.' He pointed a drumstick at my aunty, who was mopping the floor near the restrooms and looked extra pleased to be doing so.

'Fuck off.'

He tipped over his bucket, pouring bones and crusted chicken skin onto the table. Then he held out the bucket to me. 'You might want to keep this. It'll come in handy in a few years when you're living on the streets.'

'Fuck off!'

I turned my attention to the thigh pieces, chomping down on them, as if worries about the future might also be masticated into digestible mouthfuls. Raj distracted himself by playing Snake on his Nokia. Eventually, I licked my fingers clean. He looked up from the screen. 'Stupid fucking Bitch Fingers.'

I needed a break from him and got up to use the restroom. Once inside I had to use the third cubicle; someone had badly misjudged the bowl in the first, while the second was blocked with toilet paper.

Me and my aunty made eye contact as I left the toilets. She gave me another big smile. I watched her mop closer and closer to the men's restroom. I imagined her cleaning up someone else's shit with a smile on her face.

I rounded the corner and couldn't believe it: Raj had propped the empty bucket on his head. It drooped low over his eyes, limiting the range of his vision. It was kind of sad when you thought about it. He grinned at me from beneath the rim.

TALIA MARSHALL

Learning How to Behave

Driving to the tangi on the syrupy new road through Kaiapoi
I'm listening to Drake sing (I know)
but I'm a good girl, I know I'm a good girl, come on
we're going home

The good girl part of the song
isn't true so I feel it as a truth, the kind of sentiment
I used to cherish in Golden Books, *Three Little Pigs* was the best
Golden Book but what happened to the wolf?

Hohua, the newest slave, turned the wind
towards the palisades for his captors
and after the fire destroyed Kaiapoi Pa
the ash covering the corpses let him rise free
but who would want to be that kind of phoenix?

Not me

Jesse says if you say our surname in Tuahiwi
his aunties curse us with their spit on the floor
I can see why they would hate us
but I'm already at the border north of Kaikōura
between the us and the us
they turned into a them

First the house is made of straw
and then the whare is made of rain

The next house is made of sticks
asking the matches its own question with a hiss

I have a brick in my hand, it's not for building nothing
it's my heart beating itself to nowhere

It sings I am the ochre, I am the clay

I overheard Mugwi saying *that girl needs to learn how to behave*
he is right but he's also dead
I am a good girl who doesn't know what to do with all the red

I wonder if Haua, Mugwi's first name, is short for Hohua
but he was another uncle in another alphabet
and being a good girl is lame so who wants my limp?

Who isn't named after something or someone else?
I was named after the credits of *Rocky*
because my mother was sitting in the dark mouth of the movie theatre
and liked the rise and fall of Adrian's first name

My father said *call her Kahu*
and then he said nothing to us for years
but the sound of the *ah* is the same

I came after the after
after the after
which poses so well for the now
and the three little pigs
grow bigger and bigger
they love their whare so much
their fear might burst through my skin as fur

I am not a good girl, I know this
I know I am the she wolf I used to know
crying *let me in, let me in!*
I'll be a good girl, I promise

These worn yellow nubs are all that is left of my fangs

VICTOR RODGER

Night Fill

Exterior (EXT): BRIGHTON BEACH/BRIGHTON PIER, CHRISTCHURCH, NIGHT

A full moon burns brightly in the clear night sky. Silence, except for the moonlit waves gently lapping against the pillars of Brighton Pier. The beach is deserted.

EXT: BRIGHTON MALL, NIGHT

The mall is still and eerily silent. An Obama-style painting of Gerry Brownlee on a wall proclaims NOPE (instead of HOPE). Below the painting lies a pile of RUBBLE, a leftover from the earthquakes. A BLACK CAT negotiates its way over the rubble then suddenly FREEZES. It can sense something—or is it someone? The cat hisses ...

CUT TO:

EXT: SUPERMARKET, NIGHT

Through the window a handful of CUSTOMERS can be seen wandering the aisles, lit by harsh fluorescent lights.

Interior (INT): SUPERMARKET, NIGHT—MONTAGE

Bored CHECKOUT OPERATORS scan items, brains rotting. EASY LISTENING MUSIC plays.

CHECKOUT OPERATOR (voice over): The supermarket is now closed. Please make your way to the checkout counter with your items. Thank you.

INT: SUPERMARKET STORAGE ROOM, NIGHT

The night-fill manager, GORETTI (fifties, Samoan, frangipani flower in her ear), is overseeing two new staff members: VIN (18, PALAGI, nervy and uncertain) and STANZA (18, cocky stoner PALAGI). You can tell GORETTI was a looker in her day. But right now she looks world-weary as she watches a nervous VIN try to ram a pallet jack into a pallet loaded with PLASTIC-WRAPPED BOXES.

GORETTI (under her breath): Bloody hell. (To Vin): Ia, give it another go, uh?

VIN tries to ram the pallet jack into the pallet again.

GORETTI: C'mon, shove it right in there, son. You show that pallet jack who's the boss.

VIN tries again. Fails.

STANZA: Fahhhh, shame.

GORETTI: Stan, why don't you give it a go?

STANZA: It's Stanza, yo.

GORETTI: Ia, whatever you call yourself—get in there. Yo.

STANZA: A'ite.

STANZA does a slow gangsta stroll towards the pallet, tries to mimic GORETTI with the pallet jack ... but he can't fit it into the pallet either, no matter how hard he tries.

STANZA: Must be stuffed.

GORETTI: Yo. Let me show you.

STANZA (under his breath): Lame.

GORETTI: Huh?

STANZA: Nuthin'.

GORETTI takes a run-up, then expertly rams the pallet jack into the pallet.

GORETTI: Just like that. See? This old girl's still got it.

STANZA (under his breath): Got what? Arthritis?

GORETTI: O lea? (WHAT?)

STANZA: What?

GORETTI: Did you say something?

STANZA: Nah.

GORETTI pumps up the pallet jack then begins to pull the heavy pallet up a slope as the boys look on.

GORETTI: Well, don't just stand there. Give us a push.

STANZA rolls his eyes at VIN as they help push the pallet up the slope.

INT: SUPERMARKET, NIGHT

GORETTI pulls the pallet through the plastic flaps of the storage room, with STANZA and VIN in tow. VIN gets caught in the flaps and panics as he tries to free himself. STANZA sniggers. GORETTI looks at him with disgust then focuses on expertly navigating the pallet around CUSTOMERS and various displays. As she pushes past the different aisles, she introduces VIN and STANZA to the other NIGHT-FILL STAFF.

AISLE 1:

GORETTI: That's Tanz ...

TANZ *(fifties, MĀORI, looks like she came out of the womb smoking) is on her knees, using her box cutter to open a box of chocolate bars. She's about to put some bags on the shelf when a FAT GAMER (twenties, PALAGI) suddenly stands in front of her, his arse right in her face. TANZ catches a whiff of something unpleasant emanating from the FAT GAMER. She grimaces.*

AISLE 2:

GORETTI: That's Chye-Ling ...

CHYE-LING *(sixties, CHINESE, a CUDDLY NANNY type) winces with pain as she kneels down to shelve some cans of flyspray. A SPOILT BRAT (late teens, PALAGI) who is busy texting doesn't see CHYE-LING and trips over her.*

CHYE-LING: You all right, love?

SPOILT BRAT: Stupid bitch.

CHYE-LING: I beg your pardon?

SPOILT BRAT doesn't answer, just moves off. CHYE-LING sighs.

AISLE 3:

GORETTI: And that's Roshni ...

ROSHNI *(fifties, INDIAN) is putting some tins of corned beef on the shelf when she sees a RICH COW (forties, PALAGI) take some refrigerated goods from her basket and put them on the shelf. RICH COW and ROSHNI hold each other's gaze for a beat. RICH COW walks away, unrepentant.*

ROSHNI (sneering): Gah.

AISLE 4:

GORETTI brings the pallet to a halt.

GORETTI: Right, lads. *(She pulls out her box cutter.)* First of all, we get rid of all this business. *(She slashes at the plastic with gusto, removes it, then grabs a box of COKE.)*

GORETTI: Now I'm going to show you boys how to cut a display box for the fizzy. *(She notices STANZA is texting on his phone.)* Stanley?

STANZA: Fahhh—Stanza.

GORETTI: You just cut here, here, here and then voilà. *(She cuts expertly then rips away part of the carton so that the plastic bottles are exposed. She grabs another box.)*

Ia, okay: who wants to try?

VIN gulps in fright.

STANZA: Pussy.

STANZA grabs the box cutter and slashes the box with gusto.

GORETTI: Easy, easy.

STANZA cuts into a bottle: fizzy sprays everywhere.

VIN: Whoopsadaisy.

STANZA: Man, it's all over my Dickies.

GORETTI sighs.

INT: SUPERMARKET, NIGHT, LATER

As FAT GAMER, RICH COW and SPOILT BRAT file out with their shopping bags, GORETTI stands by the exit.

GORETTI: Night, guys.

FAT GAMER grunts as he eats a chocolate bar. SPOILT BRAT has her earphones in and fails to acknowledge GORETTI. RICH COW gives GORETTI a look of disdain.

GORETTI (under her breath): Ia, up yours too, your highness.

GORETTI walks outside and looks up at the full, hanging moon. TANZ joins her, lights up a cigarette.

TANZ: Wasn't too crazy. Considering.

They gaze at the moon.

GORETTI: The night's not over yet, love.

TANZ: How're those new fellas doing?

GORETTI: E. Look for yourself.

TANZ looks over at STANZA and VIN as they collect the trolleys in the carpark. STANZA is trying to ride on the back of a trolley until it SMASHES into the trolley in front. VIN is finding it impossible to manoeuvre his trolleys towards the supermarket and keeps veering off in all directions.

TANZ: Fuck me. Where do they get them?

GORETTI: Buggered if I know, love. Buggered if I know.

TANZ offers GORETTI a cigarette.

GORETTI: No thanks, love. Given up.

TANZ looks at her doubtfully.

GORETTI: Don't you look at me like that. I mean it this time. I'm never gonna smoke another sikaleki as long as I never. You watch me.

EXT: SUPERMARKET CARPARK, NIGHT

As VIN struggles to keep his trolleys together he hears a NOISE in the distance. He stops.

VIN: Did you hear that?

STANZA brings his trolley to a halt. Silence. Until he FARTS.

STANZA: Did you hear that?

STANZA sniggers.

INT: SUPERMARKET, NIGHT

GORETTI and TANZ look on as VIN tries to keep control of his trolleys. GORETTI marches over to him.

GORETTI: Here, move over.

GORETTI takes VIN's place and expertly manoeuvres the trolleys inside the supermarket, just as STANZA sails in on the back of a trolley, almost collecting GORETTI and TANZ.

TANZ: Watch it!

STANZA: Soz, man.

GORETTI: Right, you two: see if you can grab another pallet.

STANZA and VIN move off. TANZ looks at GORETTI sympathetically then heads back inside. GORETTI is about to lock the doors when a SMUG HIPSTER (mid-twenties, PALAGI) appears out of nowhere and startles her.

GORETTI: Bloody shit, you gave me a—

SMUG HIPSTER (interrupts): I need to grab some quinoa.

GORETTI: Sorry, love, we're shut.

SMUG HIPSTER: I'll be two secs.

GORETTI: If I let you in, then I have to let everyone in.

SMUG HIPSTER: There is no one else. C'mon, my lady'll kill me if I don't get it.

GORETTI: Can't help you, love.

SMUG HIPSTER: What time do you shut?

GORETTI: Nine.

SMUG HIPSTER: It's only just nine now.

GORETTI: Sorry.

SMUG HIPSTER: Where's the boss?

GORETTI: I'm the night-fill manager.

SMUG HIPSTER: I said the *boss*.

GORETTI: That'd be me.

SMUG HIPSTER: You're a shelf stacker.

GORETTI: A shelf stacker who isn't going to let you in.

SMUG HIPSTER: Are you serious?

GORETTI: That's right.

SMUG HIPSTER: Bitch.

GORETTI: Your wife's obviously a very lucky woman.

SMUG HIPSTER: Go fuck yourself, you wrinkled old prune.

GORETTI smiles brightly at SMUG HIPSTER.

GORETTI: You have a good night.

SMUG HIPSTER gives her the finger. GORETTI smiles even more brightly.

GORETTI (under her breath): Arsehole.

EXT. SUPERMARKET CARPARK, NIGHT

SMUG HIPSTER is on his cellphone as he storms towards his car.

SMUG HIPSTER: The old bag wouldn't let me in. You'll just have to do without the quinoa, okay? It won't kill you.

Suddenly SMUG HIPSTER hears a NOISE. He looks around but sees nothing. Just the darkness and a few empty cars.

SMUG HIPSTER: What? Look, I'll see you soon.

He's about to get into his car when he hears the NOISE again. He looks in the direction it came from, then opens his mouth to scream.

INT. SUPERMARKET, NIGHT

VIN is slowly navigating a pallet full of alcohol through the supermarket when he catches it on the corner of a beer display.

STANZA: Too fast, too furious.

CHYE-LING sees that the beer display is about to topple over.

CHYE-LING: Shitsticks. Girls! Aisle 2!

CHYE-LING grimaces as she gets to her feet and rushes towards the tottering beer display. TANZ and ROSHNI appear and help CHYE-LING keep the beer from falling, just as GORETTI appears.

GORETTI: Here, move aside.

GORETTI takes over from VIN and expertly steers the pallet away from the beer. CHYE-LING, TANZ and ROSHNI upright the tilting beer display while STANZA and VIN look on.

GORETTI: Well done, ladies.

TANZ, CHYE-LING, ROSHNI and GORETTI all look witheringly at STANZA and VIN.

INT. SUPERMARKET, NIGHT, MOMENTS LATER

GORETTI is putting away some toilet spray when she overhears STANZA and VIN.

STANZA (voice over): Wish we were working with some hotties instead of a bunch of old nanas.

VIN (voice over): That's mean.

STANZA (voice over): Fahhhh, it's like Jurassic Park around here.

INT. SUPERMARKET BATHROOM, NIGHT

GORETTI looks at herself in the mirror as she washes her face. She takes in all the lines on her face.

INT. SUPERMARKET BREAK ROOM, NIGHT

GORETTI, TANZ, CHYE-LING and ROSHNI are having a coffee.

TANZ: Fucking little shits. Should've just let all that beer fall and made them clean it up themselves.

CHYE-LING winces as she gingerly takes a seat.

GORETTI: How's your hip?

CHYE-LING: Still at the bottom of the waiting list.

TANZ: God, getting old is shit.

GORETTI: Sometimes I wonder if I'm getting too old for all this.

ROSHNI: Goretti, you do a great job.

CHYE-LING: We all do.

TANZ: And you're not fucking old.

ROSHNI: You know what they say, uh? You're only as old as the man you feel.

TANZ: Dirty bitch.

The women laugh, then they hear an ALMIGHTY CRASH.

INT. SUPERMARKET, NIGHT

GORETTI, TANZ, ROSHNI and CHYE-LING stand at the foot of a mountain of broken beer bottles.

GORETTI (under her breath): Bloody shit. Boys! Boys?

VIN and STANZA pop their heads out from behind a fridge in the distance.

GORETTI: What're you boys doing back there?

STANZA looks alarmed, puts a finger to his mouth as if to say 'shhh' then points behind GORETTI. GORETTI follows STANZA's gaze. It's SMUG HIPSTER, lurching down an aisle. But he looks a lot different now. Paler. Bloodier. In fact, just like a ZOMBIE.

GORETTI: How the hell did you get in here?

SMUG HIPSTER continues to lurch forwards.

STANZA: I think he's a zombie, Goretti.

GORETTI: I don't give a bloody shit what he is. Oi: Hairy McClary: I already told you—we're shut.

SMUG HIPSTER keeps coming.

GORETTI: If you don't get out of here I'm calling the cops.

When SMUG HIPSTER lurches even closer, GORETTI pulls out her phone. SMUG HIPSTER suddenly lunges at her but she easily side-steps him. He lunges at her again. This time he grabs GORETTI and tries to bite her face off.

CHYE-LING: Shitsticks!

ROSHNI: Get off her, you hairy hairy!

TANZ, CHYE-LING and ROSHNI pull SMUG HIPSTER off GORETTI while STANZA and VIN look on.

GORETTI (sarcastic): It's all right, boys—you just stay where you are.

SMUG HIPSTER falls against a row of pasta sauces, which CRASH to the floor. Sauce SPLATTERS everywhere.

CHYE-LING: Bloody hell, I just put those out.

SMUG HIPSTER gets to his feet and grabs ROSHNI. GORETTI pulls out her box cutter and STABS his arm. SMUG HIPSTER releases ROSHNI but doesn't seem that wounded.

STANZA: In the head!

GORETTI: O lea? (WHAT?)

STANZA: Stab him in the head.

GORETTI plunges the box cutter right into SMUG HIPSTER's temple. He falls to the ground. GORETTI, TANZ, CHYE-LING and ROSHNI encircle the dead zombie.

GORETTI: Ia, ai kae. (EAT SHIT.)

STANZA: Behind you!

The women turn. RICH COW and FAT GAMER, also now zombies, are moving towards them from the end of the aisle.

VIN: Watch out!

They turn and see a zombiefied HOT BRAT lurching towards them from the other end of the aisle. They're surrounded. The women retreat to the middle of the aisle, back to back.

GORETTI: Ready, ladies?

TANZ: Fuckin A.

ROSHNI: Bring it on.

CHYE-LING: Shitsticks.

GORETTI lets out a primal scream.

INT. SUPERMARKET, NIGHT—ZOMBIE FIGHTING MONTAGE

GORETTI slices RICH COW's stomach open with her box cutter. Her guts spill onto the floor. ROSHNI grabs two huge cans of corned beef and uses them to SMASH RICH COW's head open. CHYE-LING grabs a bottle of bleach, opens it and throws it in HOT BRAT'S face. She yelps in agony and stumbles around blindly. TANZ grabs a spade and whacks FAT GAMER across the head. He falls to the ground. TANZ continues to WHACK him until his head explodes.

TANZ: Yeah, fucker, take that!

GORETTI stabs HOT BRAT in the head with her box cutter again and again. Blood spurts everywhere. HOT BRAT falls to the ground. Covered in blood, GORETTI, TANZ, CHYE-LING and ROSHNI stand victorious among the dead bodies. VIN and STANZA cautiously emerge from behind the fridge. GORETTI wipes some blood from her face. VIN vomits. But STANZ is impressed.

STANZA: Fahhhh, you the man, Goretti. You the man.

A beat of silence.

GORETTI goes over to the cigarette stand, takes a packet from the case.

TANZ: But I thought ...

GORETTI gives TANZ a look as if to say: all bets are off. GORETTI goes to grab a lighter but STANZA beats her to it. He lights her cigarette. GORETTI takes a long drag, exhales then looks at the boys.

GORETTI: Well, don't just fucking stand there. Clean this shit up.

MAJELLA CULLINANE

Suburban Aubade

> *And here am I, budding*
> *among the ruins*
> *with only sorrow to bite on,*
> *as if weeping were a seed and I*
> *the earth's only furrow.*—Pablo Neruda

In the last years of her life my mother slept too much or didn't sleep at all. Her sleep was often broken, her dreams troubled, her grasp on the present fragile and fragmented as dementia increasingly addled her memory and sense of reality. She lost track of time and would wake in the small hours, creep downstairs and make herself a cup of tea, sit alone in the kitchen. I'd imagine her in suburban Limerick listening to the pre-dawn chorus, which she always loved, and even with the vast distance between us I'd conjure the sounds of my childhood: the buoyant robin, first to acknowledge the smallest whisper of light; the fluent, mellow notes of the blackbird; the cooing pigeon gradually joining in atop my father's old shed.

It was autumn in New Zealand when my mother died, autumn when I last saw her in Ireland. Since then, the world has been in full or partial lockdown, completely altered in a matter of months. It's as though the absurd notion I've had these twelve years living here, of the world as a kind of hourglass containing the northern and southern hemispheres within two glass bulbs—an imaginary hourglass I've often turned upside down to orientate myself to the different seasons—has been inverted over and over. Our activities and wanderings are now strictly limited; any illusory concept of time and the seasons I once had is wedged inside the hourglass's neck—suspended.

In the weeks following my mother's death I didn't sleep well. Like her, I'd wake in darkness, get up and make coffee, then sit at my desk in the corner of the sitting room. Outside the window, clematis twisted around the balcony's wooden trellis, slivers of streetlight shone through the partially opened curtains. Some mornings the rain reminded me of piano scales: a trickle of fingertips over keys, lightly touched, the notes almost unheard; on other days the rain's din was as insistent on the corrugated iron roof as a child throwing a tantrum.

Through another window I looked out at our tiny sleeping garden, traced the narrow path around its white-picket-fenced perimeter, past the pale pink rhododendron that each year shed its splendour to spring's icy southerlies, past the overgrown beds of lavender, the yellow flower of the kōwhai that had bloomed early. In between the path's square slabs, sow thistle pushed through relentlessly, not unlike the many South Islanders I've met in the years since moving here, who consider themselves staunch and tough, persistent and hardy.

On mid-autumn mornings after a hard frost the sun suffused each moment with light, the air was stiller, sharper. On the neighbour's oak tree, tawny leaves clung precariously to a mesh of increasingly bare branches. On mornings such as these I listened attentively to the unique phrasing of two birds, the melodious bellbird and tūī that hold court over the dawn chorus. Two lead singers in a band otherwise comprising non-native vocalists such as the blackbird and thrush, introduced to New Zealand by the Acclimatisation Society in the 1860s and 70s.

The bellbird or korimako, whose plumage and colour differ depending on what part of the country you find them in, has twenty-six different names in te reo Māori to reflect individual iwi (tribal) descriptions. In the 'deep south', as TV meteorologists like to call this part of the South Island, they are found in orchards, gardens and parks and along riverbanks. Apart from noticing them in the neighbour's oak, I have heard their remarkable, bell-like song as they delve into the fuchsia and camellias in our garden, busily imbibing nectar with their brush-tipped tongues.

Until recently I'd never seen a bellbird up close. I had thought them shy and reticent until I spotted one on a small shrub beside a busy road near the university. Its mossy green breast was distinctive, its manner of rotating itself up and around to get at a flower suggestive of a trapeze artist or a gymnast. In my surprise, I uttered 'bellbird' aloud. It was so close I could have reached out and touched it. The korimako song also has regional variations, but always consists of loud, clear and liquid ringing notes.

When we first moved south from the Kāpiti Coast in 2015 I told my partner's mother, a keen birdwatcher, that I thought I'd heard a bellbird in our garden. She asked: 'Are you sure it's a bellbird and not a tūī?' A renowned mimic of birds and humans, the tūī possesses two voice boxes, which facilitate a range of song encompassing ornate, fluid melodies in combination with a recurrent assortment of coughs, clicks, grunts, wheezes, chortles and creaks. A Māori proverb describes great orators or singers as 'me he korokoro tūī', which means having 'the throat of a tūī.' Given the birds' facility for imitation, early Māori also considered tūī messengers and mediums to aid communication with the gods.

After over a decade in New Zealand I find their song still fascinates me. It is like nothing I'd ever heard previously. Given their tendency for loquaciousness, it's perhaps unsurprising that tūī are considered more rambunctious than their fellow nectar-eaters, bellbirds. While it may be rare to see a bellbird at close range, tūī are boisterous and energetic. From a distance they appear black, but up close they have a greenish-teal, midnight-blue sheen. On their throat a lacy collar of white feathers, which is why early European settlers called them parson birds. More accurate would be the Māori description of their throat feathers resembling poi and made from balls of flax, raupō (bulrush) or white wool.

In flight tūī exhibit white shoulder patches on their wings like epaulettes; with their long broad tails they are noisy fliers, varying between short and long glides. Like bellbirds, their habitat includes native forest, scrub, farmland and suburban gardens where they feed on kōwhai, gum trees and red kahikatea berries. Notoriously belligerent, they will defend their territory from other tūī, even if it is only a small part of a larger tree. Their loud, whirring wings in combination with their sporadic, theatrical divebombs and flamboyant calls are enough to deter other birds, including the dainty native fantail and flocking waxeye.

Like bellbirds, tūī song dialect is regionally variant, and much of it inaudible to the human ear. As Stephanie Chamberlain writes in *New Zealand Geographic*: '[T]ūī song brings a poignant companionship to clear autumn days, providing a mellow soundtrack to these quieter moments.' With tūī and the euphonious bellbird providing the soundtrack for these mornings alone in the sitting room, autumnal light plays its part too. As the minutes slip by on one such morning, the sky is furrowed with innuendos of colour—over the hills a dusty lavender that gently nudges its way to a tender lapis, and then, towards dawn, the signature opal blue of a clear-skied, icy day.

My sister lives in rural County Clare where phone and internet reception are patchy and intermittent. On her way to work and at weekends she phones me on WhatsApp. As she drives, her voice often breaks up and I catch only part of a sentence; we're frequently cut off. It's better when she's stationary, when she's parked her car or stands in front of the cream-painted bungalow she calls home. She calls me more now that neither one of us can speak to our mother, checking to see how I am. We've not long reached the stage where we can speak about her without crying.

One morning my sister called and told me the weather was mild there, that they were expecting temperatures into the high teens. She wasn't long up she said and still in her pyjamas. We talked for a few moments about this and that, then she paused and told me a robin (*an spideog* in Irish) had come close to the car. She said, 'You know what that means, don't you?' I was aware of some superstitions about robins from my mother: that should one fly into your house through an open window there will be a death; that the robin was present at Christ's crucifixion and, flying too close to the crown of thorns pricked its breast, which was how it became red; that bad luck will follow you if you intentionally harm a robin or its blue eggs.

I had not heard what my sister then told me: that robins were also said to carry the spirits of deceased loved ones, and appeared especially when they were near. I later read that robins are supposedly a sign from heaven, and can transport messages indicating, for example, that a loved one is at peace. My mother's favourite bird was the robin and she always fed them when they came to the back door for breadcrumbs. Not only was she lulled by their quavering, sometimes bright, occasionally melancholic song, but there was something that she perhaps identified with in their courage to come so close, their robustness despite their size. The robin approached the world with the smallest measure of expectation, just as she had attempted to, despite the challenges and difficulties of her childhood.

Having said this, I think my mother would have had a good laugh at my sister's imagining her spirit transmogrifying into a robin. She would have teased her for being 'soft in the head' but she'd have also understood, like me, that as illogical and outlandish as superstitions are, they offer consolation to the bereaved.

I wonder what my mother would have made of the bellbird and tūī, of the birdsong unique to this country she never visited, these sounds that are still marvellously exotic to my ear; the acoustic prologue and epilogue to my day; a gentle reminder that I am far from where I came from.

In Philip Larkin's poem 'Aubade' he writes about waking in the early hours of the morning with an intense dread. Terrified by the inevitability and unknowability of what lies after death, he views any bravery in the face of it as ultimately futile. While the approaching light signifies the relentlessness of death—'a whole day nearer now'—there is, I'd suggest, the subtlest hope in the final lines of the poem: as 'slowly light strengthens, and the room takes shape', and although 'the sky is white as clay, with no sun', 'work has to be done'. The poet has ultimately accepted that despite his fear of death, there is nothing to do but to get on with the business of living.

Larkin's pre-dawn terror is reminiscent of the seventeenth-century theologian and historian Thomas Fuller, who wrote: '[I]t is always darkest just before the day dawneth'; and analogous to what Swedish film director Ingmar Bergman called 'the hour of the wolf'. 'The hour which occurs between night and dawn. The hour when most people die, when sleep is deepest, when nightmares are most real.' It was in these hours that my mother struggled to breathe, and finally died, just before dawn.

As each night relinquishes to a new day, the light can assuage our fears, even if only momentarily. Irrespective of how transitory, the dawn embodies the idea of new beginnings. It announces the undeniable fact that Larkin recoiled from, that despite death and our fear of non-existence, life will continue without us. The natural world will not notice; the time I envisage as suspended or inverted in my imaginary hourglass will slip through regardless.

And yet, even with the experience of intense grief, by observing the sky retreat from darkness, there is solace in listening to birdsong. Confronted with sleeplessness and sorrow, we can gradually lean into the light that kindles their distinctive voices and calls; we can attempt to endure that breach of self that emanates from loss. Although my mother will not be there to welcome me when I next return to Limerick, there will still be robin song, the cooing pigeon, and even the cacophonous crow that she never liked; the aubade of another suburban home, a little something unchanged in the life we once shared.

References

Heather Barrie & Hugh Robertson, *Field Guide to the Birds of New Zealand*, Auckland: Oxford University Press, 1997

Murdoch Riley, *Manu Māori: Bird legends and customs*, Wellington: Viking Sevenseas NZ Ltd, 2006

Stephanie Chamberlin, 'Tui', *New Zealand Geographic*: www.nzgeo.com/stories/tui/

Niall Mac Coitir, *Ireland's Birds: Myths, legends and folklore*, Ireland: The Collins Press, 2017

Philip Larkin, *Collected Poems*, London: Faber & Faber, 1988

Thomas Fuller, *A Pisgah-sight of Palestine*, Andesite Press, 2015

Ingmar Bergman, *The Hour of the Wolf* (film), 1968

J. WIREMU KANE

Polypharmacy

'Not tonight,' I type. 'I had a rough day.' The phone screen blurs in and out of focus but I always manage to send coherent sentences. 'I just washed down a Temazepam with Johnnie Walker Red.' Nearly always. Temazepam is mustard yellow and blended Scotch is amber. 'I wouldn't be much fun to be around.'

'Andy'll pick you up on his way there.' When did that message arrive? 'You can just take it easy.'

I'll take it easy in the crush of Emilia's flat with the undersized deck and its untamed garden filling with barbecue smoke.

I'll probably look quiet. Reserved. Tired.

He's a doctor, you know, someone will probably say. It's a tough job.

He looked so sad. His eyes too big and too brown. Baby rabbit eyes. Bambi eyes.

'You made it!' Emilia acts as if she hasn't organised my ride. Her eyes are kind. The left one wrinkles more than the right when she's amused. He's so stoned, I imagine her saying to Andy when I'm out of earshot. He thinks we can't tell.

Benzos and booze. Two sedatives that can be deadly when combined, but I know what I'm doing. Sort of. I know my body: it's frightening what it can handle. How rapidly tolerance builds. How rapidly that could become a problem if I let it.

But I won't let it.

I know what I'm doing.

'Oh, hi, Wiri,' my colleague with the brown eyes said. He was carefully positioned behind the 'Staff Only' line, though he spoke as though we were passing in the corridor. He was not wearing his glasses and looked blind without them. 'Can you tell me what's going on?'

I knew when it was time to prove I could stop.

I stayed awake all day and all night and all day and all night.

I had to pee every five minutes. Thoughts galloped, thundered. Hooves churned up the electrified blob of fat, screaming for gamma aminobutyric acid.

Gimme! Please? Just a little flow of chloride ions?

Bladder doubles in on itself. One desperate drop comes out.

Drink more water, kidney scolds.

Let me sleep.

Not worth flushing the toilet for that.

'None of us here can treat you.' My voice was somewhere between friend and doctor. Warmth, with an edge of professional distance. 'We all know you too well.'

Hour thirteen of attempted sobriety sounds like a Well-Tempered Clavier—mathematics in music. Johan Sebastian was a sadist. Mechanical plucking of harpsichord and clavichord, notes tremble and I feel each individual beat of the vibrating air. I never properly understood wave forms until now.

Please let me sleep.

I barely knew him. Rumours of bullying by another junior doctor. Bully's eyes, too, were brown, but pale and watery. He didn't seem like the type to torture a colleague. He laughed too loud, drank too much—but didn't we all. A good keen Kiwi bloke, reassuring and one of the boys, he spoke with a down-to-earth, working-class accent. (No less put on than my own doctor voice. Careful, rounded vowels. Deliberate Rs and Ts on any words that might be unclear. Not a trace of brown in my speech. A surprise when people meet me face to face.

'Oh, Wiri! Sorry, I thought you said Willy over the phone.' Then what? Handshake? Hongi? Cheek kiss?

'You don't look like a doctor / You don't look Māori.'

Odd, because I am a doctor, I am Māori, and this is what I look like.

Too aggressive. Be the model minority. Smile and pretend it's fine ...)

'We have to transfer you to Rotorua Hospital.' I handed him a list of the doctors at the inpatient unit there. 'They all say they haven't worked with you, but can you check this list to make sure, please?'

It is too hot, too noisy in the meagre shade of the cramped deck.

Thick air settles at the base of the wide, shallow bowl of the Waikato. My Indigenous hair frizzes. The roar of the cicadas pulls me back to the cacophonous summer we found the dead tūī. Its partner called out for it every day. The same patient, plaintive tone in perfect 7/8 time.

'Toot toot toot toot! Toot toot toot!'

J.S. Bach was too much of a formalist ever to use that time signature.

'Toot toot toot toot! Toot toot toot!'

It's the sound I wake up to and the last I hear as I struggle to sleep. Like a referee's whistle. Aotearoa Gothic against the background of the persistent whine of the tarakihi or cicadas.

'Tara ra-ta kita kita!'

Your brain tunes out, only for it to surge back at full volume when you least expect it. Screaming my name.

'Wiri o papa towene towene!'

'Wiri!'

'*Wiri!*'

It would've been dramatic. House of God *style.*

It would've gone overlooked in the news. A small story about an incident in the hospital multi-storey carpark.

Coded language for those who know.

On a clear day, when the whole world is in deep focus, the almost perfect cone of Te Aroha and the scribbled lines where the Coromandels meet the Kaimais looked close enough to touch.

From up that high you could even see a bright glow of white reflecting off the glaciers of Ruapehu. Ice that gouged its way down the mountain and, against all odds, flowed in lazy loops around the base of the hill the hospital was built on.

The hospital ...

'Sorry.' What was I apologising for this time? I got in the car with the rest of the Johnnie Walker Red. Black is nicer but Red is cheaper. Temazepam is yellow and Zopiclone is blue and Lorazepam 1mgs are tiny and white with a line down the middle you can bite in half but you always get 0.65mg or 0.35mg and never actually half, and they taste of lactose.

'You okay?' Andy always speaks too quietly.

'Yup.'

'You wanna stop somewhere? Grab some mixers for that? Or something for the barbie?'

'What? Oh, no thanks, I'm fine. I had a pie from … you know, the dairy around the corner.'

I composed an email in my head: 'I'm still having trouble sleeping which further escalates my anxiety. I will only use Temazepam at night for sleep as a last resort. Please fax the prescription to Anglesea Pharmacy so I can pick it up after work …'

Thirty tablets *mitte*.

Mitte. Latin for send. Only. No more than. A frowning mouth scrawled at the bottom of the script. How much Latin have I picked up? It's important that our patients cannot always understand us. We need a secret language, one thought long dead.

Mitte means no more.

Thirty tablets ONLY.

Potential for abuse.

May cause drowsiness.

Bad for operating cranes but okay to reassure a colleague and sort-of-friend and not-really-patient that he'll be okay.

To type a hasty discharge summary without lingering on details.

To hang a mostly unneeded stethoscope around my neck as a badge of honour.

'No, you see I *work* here.'

He looked weird without his stethoscope around his neck. Still in his dress shirt and trousers. Untucked. No shoes. Had he taken them off and left them up where the security guard found him? Or were they taken from him, the laces removed? His black hair ruffled. His big, pretty eyes unframed.

A glance across the ward.

Patient alert and active, *I typed.*

He said he was not sure what he planned to do up there. Whether he'd intended to jump or not. He can't remember. No, he didn't want to die, but yes, he is struggling.

Able to answer questions.

He looked so sad ...

In no apparent distress.

I watched him walk over to where some other patients were playing pool and doing jigsaw puzzles. Wasgij puzzles.

Neurologic exam, grossly normal.

I moved my stethoscope across his chest. A stylised Z covering aortic, pulmonic, tricuspid and mitral areas.

Heart sounds 1 + 2 + nil.

I sip neat whiskey and don't listen to the chatter or the Spotify playlist of basic bro tunes while the tūī toots along to minuets and bagatelles. My sweat-soaked back sticks to the worn brown leather of the couch. There's just enough room for someone to sit next to me. No one sits next to me.

Living situation: Single. Lives with flatmates. Family back in Malaysia.

We all know the type. All friends are work friends. Minimum sixty hours a week. Working every second or third weekend. Twelve work days in a row. Thirty of the forty-eight hours of the weekend on your feet. A full work week still to suffer through.

Any wonder the days smear and smudge together with or without chemical help.

Friendships are fragile. Friable as the veins of the arachnoid mater that stretch, tear and ooze. When you turn down or bail on social plans nine times out of ten, there isn't often an eleven.

A reminder alarm sounds on my phone as I type up his notes.

Fuck, there's that fucking barbecue tonight ...

Midazolam 7.5mg tablets are white, oval cylindrical, biconvex. The shiny outer coating is sweeter than sugar. A foil packet that could be ibuprofen or paracetamol at first glance. Why would anyone bother taking a second?

Working-class bully man should've known better. He should've been his friend. His family. Sixty hours a week minimum together. Dividing up the tasks. Dividing up the patients. You soon learn the best ways of working together—who prefers paperwork to procedures, who is more confident to make referrals, to ask the bosses questions, to present cases, to place IVs ...

You learn to track each other's moods, notice trends—increased despondency, complaints of tiredness that go beyond the usual. Irritability. Lack of concentration. Changes in posture. Fewer smiles and laughs.

Signs we're trained to look out for. Signs that can be misused—handing over admissions to others. Not completing paperwork.

'Hey, man, I need to leave on time today, so can you do that catheter for me?' in that blokey, man-of-the-people drawl we all know is fake. 'That cannula? That discharge summary?'

Easy to be lazy and selfish. He should've known better. Been better. Shouldn't we all.

Venlafaxine are dark red, and green is green with an odour that wrinkles noses and attracts wry, knowing looks. Stop looking at me like that; it'll be legal soon. You're not clever and I've never claimed to be cool.

We're always tired. We're nearly always miserable. We all have the same coping mechanisms.

Most of us turn inward. Blame ourselves. Abuse ourselves.

Everyone else is coping, why can't you?

If they're not letting their weaknesses show, why are you?

It must be a relief to externalise it, to project it all onto someone else—partners, kids, workmates. But I never could, and neither could my friend with the sad eyes.

He doesn't explain himself and I don't need him to.

My brow furrows. Muscles immediately protest: Why did you make us do that? What do you even want from us?

Myosin proteins slide along actin. A caterpillar kinking its way along a long leaf. False colour electron microscope animations that are just as representative as illustrations where arteries are red, veins are blue, nerves are yellow, and lymphatics are green. Anatomy is Gray and god I hate myself for that one.

'What's funny?' Emilia asks.

'Huh?'

'Your face was doing that thing where you're laughing inside.' Her eyes are kind and the left one crinkles ...

I see why I thought you had to be a doctor to observe people. We're the only ones who claim to be gods. Maybe you have to be a dick to be a doctor. There must be easier ways to be worshipped. We're all just failed cult leaders, looking to be adored.

I got into medicine because I want to help people!

No, you wanted magic letters in front of and behind your name that command immediate respect. Respect that you and your ancestors clawed and scraped to get, broken nails bleeding and coated in dust while indifferent boots stomped and stomped.

And you're a wave, smashing yourself apart again and again and again against adamantium cliffs: 'But haven't you done so well to get where you are, um ... am I saying your name right?'

You are the future of this country. You are your ancestors' wildest dreams. You are a bright, shining symbol we can hold up and push to the front of group photos, make sure that bone carving around your neck is showing.

You're called Wir ... Wir ... WirEmu. Be sure to use that whenever possible. It looks much better in print than Dr Bastardised-Irish-Surname.

He didn't try to explain himself and I didn't need him to.

But I was glad he was alive.

A cloud passes over Emilia's face. Her head is turned so shadows carve a crescent off her face. A waning, gibbous moon.

I tense up inside. On the surface I barely react. A mild shrug of depolarisation.

You did this to us, my muscles say. What did you expect?

The tarakihi resume their shrieking in my head.

The ghost of the mourning tūī joins them.

Taut strings perform aerobatics.

She's going to do it. She's going to ask if I'm okay or something like that. I can already feel the corners of my eyes pricking, my chest constricting. Outwardly nothing continues to happen.

My brain lets off a few sparks. Wasn't this your goal? it shrugs. Not just blunted affect, blunted everything.

Wiri o papa towene towene!

Quiver your hindquarters!

Though I guess it could also be translated as 'Shake dat ass! Shake dat ass!'

'You're doing it again.' Emilia's eyes are kind. 'What's funny?'

'It's too—'

You're not gonna attempt circuitous in your state, are you? Brain cocks an eyebrow.

'—convoluted to try and explain.' I still manage to sound pretentious. 'And not actually very funny.'

'Okay. We'll see you tomorrow, right?'

'What's tomorrow?'

'Brunch. We were thinking around 10.30. Andy said he could give you a ride again.'

When you turn down or bail on plans nine times out of ten, there isn't—

'Yeah, sounds good.' My phone is in my hand, my fingers moving ahead of my brain. 'I'll set an alarm right now so I don't forget.'

Whoever art-directed my tragicomedy is a hack. The hospital on the only hill for fucking miles looms over my flat. I can see it from my bedroom. I can see it from the lounge. Not from the bathroom, which has no windows but an inadequate extractor fan.

At least I can't see the carpark building. But I can imagine. I know too much about the human body and its limitations. I can picture it too clearly. Broken. Bloody. Blood is dark red—always a darker shade than you imagine as it spreads across black asphalt.

No.

No. No.

Too far. He didn't do it. You don't need to picture how it would've ...

Lorazepam 1mg are tiny and white and taste of lactose. The smell of green tends to cling to hands, to your breath, to your clothes, and I can't care.

'Do you have anyone who can bring you some clothes and toiletries and stuff to take with you?'

'I ... I don't ...'

'That's fine I'll get someone to sort something out.'

His too big, too brown, too sad eyes focused on the floor.

I just wanted to see them bright and full of life. I just wanted to hug him, to pull him close, let him bury his face in my chest and let it absorb his heaving sobs while I stroked his back.

I just wanted to tell him it would all be fine.

I don't remember what I ended up saying. It was probably kind but professional, my smooth, breezy, most importantly *non-threatening* voice. If we're supposed to become what we pretend to be, Kurt Vonnegut, why, why the fuck can I not? Why can I not be the smooth, confident, unruffled doctor I outwardly present?

Can I not ...

I open the email saved to my drafts. I delete it and request an appointment instead. I resist the urge to clear my alarm.

It's a step.

Venlafaxine are dark red, and green is green with an odour that wrinkles noses and attracts wry looks. Lorazepam 1mg tablets are still tiny, white, and still taste like lactose.

'And that prescription has lasted you a whole year?' Dr Walker asks when he sees me.

I nod.

We both know how easy it is.

Anyone's prescribing can be audited, but they usually aren't. Lots of drug rooms have entry codes; you don't even have to swipe your trackable ID. No cameras at that end of the corridor.

Once a registrar handed me a loaded syringe of morphine.

'Chuck that in the sharps bin for me, Wiri?' There was nothing to stop me slipping it into my pocket. Slipping it into a vein.

No wonder we make such good drug addicts. I've tightened countless tourniquets around arms and palpated crooks of elbows, feeling thick, springy veins bounce around below papery skin.

'Make a fist for me, please. Relax and squeeze.' Blood butts up against the collapsed vein. Swab with an alcohol wipe. Let it dry. Feel the tension give way as the needle slips in and blood bubbles into the flashback. Release the tourniquet. Blood is dark red. Always darker than you expect.

Why wouldn't he be in the drug room? I imagine nurses, orderlies, other doctors thinking. He has the magic talisman around his neck. The magic letters before and after his name.

It's a tough job.

He knows what he's doing.

30 tablets, the script says.

Mitte.

Only.

Enough.

I didn't keep the syringe of morphine, but I could've.

TRISHA HANIFIN

Without the Scaffold of Words

At night my body lies across
the dark animal of sleep
my mind floodlit with memories

Images bloom expanding
like stars, then fade without
the scaffold of words

All day I've tried to describe my mother
the way even at eighty
her face opened like a girl's

Between image and speech is a gap
small, swiftly closed, so saturated
with light I capture nothing

What remains is a vibration
in the space she's abandoned
and this going down into silence.

LILY HOLLOWAY

periphery

there is a blur   on the edge
of the rockpool   on
the surface of a taut and
under-hanging   globe
of green   there are fish
suspended   in their darting
under your shadow
children hiding   in the
cupboards and archways
your mass has laid down

I didn't know who you were at this point
I purged you afterwards
but there you are

a knee in the corner   a hand on the
breakfast table   not even just an empty
silhouette—this might have been
okay—but a flurry   of
wings a hiss
of bus   at stoplight
the breaking   of thick
pottery   I have been here for
years   and I know
it will never be home

you're standing over
standing over my river
in the same spot   each time

around

Under the Falling Chestnuts

The children
in the swimming hole.
The fields
slick with rain.

The piglet
under greenhouse peastraw
hiding from Jock
who lives in the caravan

who might be an angel
taking breath here
under the falling chestnuts.
Your bottle-green raincoat

runs amid the lilies
feet through fallen plums.
Flee from the barn
past the woodpile

to the DOC walkway
under the mountains,
my grandfather's joy.
He will tell me

about the flood
when Dad was young,
boulders grinding
along the bed

and the games of war
hidden in mossy hollows
in the small divots
required for bodies.

There is such resting now.
We have our Vogel's
where a tree trunk lies
on the curve of the Anatoki
while around us
the generals
and pīwakawaka
spark off.

CLAUDIA JARDINE

Field Notes on Elegy

a downside to being a fairly competent singer
is that no one has ever serenaded me
and how i love poor singers!
no matter how toneless
i am your best friend at karaoke
yet it is one thing to sing along with something on the radio
or follow the creep of colour and language in the foreground
of a stranger's holiday in Rome or Nepal and quite another
to stand still
lungs full of breath
swallowing one's heart

when we were seated at the dinner
i said i was leaving
no one got to their feet

try not to think the ancient thoughts
but in my head there was *always* something ancient about this
as if years ago our ancestors met at a dusty table
and agreed

i was writing myself into scenes that were not happening
casting my eyes across rooms we were not in
standing jilted
in the doorway or on the stairs of a dark and over-furnished country house
in a fucking empire silhouette dress
just to enhance the embarrassment of feeling
i was reading poems about *a haunted wheelbarrow*
and *walking over glass // to reach the other man*

imagining myself a hopeless Roman writhing on a chaise longue
legs supported and wits adrift
or the Lady of Shalott
catching sight of my cracked reflection across the room
all for Lancelot and his *tirra lirra*
my weaving ruined

... sī nōstri̵ ōblītă tăcērĕt
sāna̵ ēssēt. nūnc quōd gānnĭt ĕt ōblŏquĭtŭr
nōn sōlūm mĕmĭnīt sēd quaē mūlto̵ ācrĭŏr ēst rēs
īrāta̵ est. hōc ēst ūrĭtŭr ēt lŏquĭtŭr.

if she were silent, so forgetful of us,
she could be sane: now she grumbles and interrupts
because she not only remembers but, what is more dazzling,
she is furious. that's it, she burns and she speaks.

i walk amid the altars until my name feels like a dactyl again
play the spaniel under the table at a great feast
placing my big heavy head in the laps of family and friends

feed sacred chickens and hope for good news

Catullus was a lil' bitch who put too much trust in being read
but if one was to ask Sulpicia, Sempronia, Clodia, Sappho,
what do you think they would say?

when we do meet i lose my mind for a minute
briefly consider painting my name on a little boat
and staging my own death
float downriver just to hear you call me *fair*

patience and ferocity
what would my namesake think?
kept awake at night by so many lyres being restrung

hoping for the sound of footsteps in the garden

and if sincerity frightens you
tough luck
i am below your window
chewing on my tender thoughts
like Atthis in her fragment, shining and
conspicuous

you don't have to look
you don't have to listen
but the karaoke machine will get here soon and
that might make things difficult

This work features several lines of Catullus 83, both in the original Latin and translated into English by the author. The poem also references 'Monica' by Hera Lindsay Bird, 'Sabina, and the Chain of Friendship' by Anna Jackson, 'The Lady of Shalott' by Lord Alfred Tennyson and Sappho fragment 96. Sulpicia and Sappho were two of the foremost poets of antiquity, Sempronia was depicted in the *Bellum Catilinae* of Sallust, and Clodia is widely believed to be one of the subjects of Catullus' poetry.

PHILIP ARMSTRONG

Beyond the Pleasure Principle

If anybody asked—they never do—
my notion of utopia I'd say
it's drinking coffee in a foreign city
where people are speaking softly
a language I don't know, which sounds
like blackbirds' songs, too complex to mean
nothing and no two phrases the same.

If you asked—but why would you?—my concept
of the good life, I'd tell you the first eight
minutes of a film: someone pegs out
underwear, their day's work done, follows
the dog down a shady lane, feeds soup
to a mother in fadeout; the part before
the part beyond which nothing is the same.

The young guy at the counter smiles and asks
me what I'd like. Straight off, instead
of words my mind goes to the sound of wind
through trees, a finger held to lips,
the intricate wood closing like a box,
the night sea smoothed like a pillow.
Nothing for me, thanks all the same.

ZOË MEAGER

John Bender has come to live in Seddonville, New Zealand

It's 1986, a year after Bender joined *The Breakfast Club* and a year after he walked away from Claire Standish, pumping his fist in the air. When detention was finally over, he'd wrapped his arms around her and kissed her with near-criminal intent, and she'd pressed a single diamond stud into the palm of his grubby fingerless glove, and he thought his big hands had never held anything so precious. These days he's one of only four guys still working the Charming Creek Mine just south of Seddonville, because the burning of high-sulphur coal has become uncool; you can't do it around hospitals or schools. 1986 is also the year the mine will close, though if he knew, Bender would inform you with pointed finger *that's a fucking coincidence, man*. Bender delights in coal mining as a form of destructive rebellion. The way he does it, you'd almost call it art. But it's a fact that no matter how hard he blasts the bituminous coal, there are no more diamonds in this world for guys like Bender. He ends his shifts with a head hard as rock and eyes that see everything in shades of black. His heart, though—wrapped inside that flannel shirt inside that scorched-earth chest—his heart just won't quit thumping. Still the hydro mine keeps sluicing everything away, and the wooden buildings and even the steel-lined flume will sink in a decade or two into the airless grey-green ocean of trees. The locals adore him in that West Coast way: give him hassles, get him wasted, take him home, smoke dope and talk shit with him under corrugated plastic porches as the rain thunders down like felled wood. All around, tender nīkau shudder to the raindrops' touch. When Bender gets tight, he spits in his hand and offers it to anyone in stumbling distance, telling them *Look, real diamonds.* The locals ignore him in that West Coast way: do it with him on couches and in gauzy-draped beds, under mink blankets and the broken cocoons of unzipped sleeping bags, and in the morning cook him fresh-laid eggs. Over here, the women look deep into their dream-catchers, crystals, candles, or they look sharp at the burning end of the morning's first cigarette, and they just nod their heads to the side and blink when sometimes he calls them *Claire*. He's just another well-built guy with a whole lot of stories. Exactly the kind of guy who's always pining for something around here.

ALISON DENHAM

Heritage Roses, Northern Cemetery

No matter how well these belles of grand balls past
look, rambling over the balustrade,
how they scramble and arch to frame
a grave in red, pink, soft yellow,
divinely scenting the breeze,

no matter how newly opened buds are shown to best against
rusted iron wrought intricate as last season's lace
how tightly wound the petals, how
pleasing the high bushes shining in bee hum,
their heritage rootstock holding

them upright in pews, all along verdant
grassy corridors weaving in and out of
tree shadow and the stones at all their heads—

it was you, forever-daughter
never-wife, who whispered the warning
tale of the scarlet bud, unlucky
petals that crumble dirt brown
in your warm hand the instant
you are gone from this place ...

The letters of your name gently tapped by thorns.
No matter you say.

AMY HEAD

Outreach

One day in summer Gerald parked at the end of Willow Street, a cul-de-sac that hadn't been a cul-de-sac before the quakes. There were bollards installed to separate it from the unused stretch of road that ran along the riverside, and on the other side of the river was the red zone, fifteen hundred acres of it. Gerald pulled in, turned off the ignition and let the rumble of combustion subside. A voice on the radio told him a new complex of bars and restaurants awaited him in the city. 'Gritty' it was, apparently. Gritty didn't mean the cleaners had left concrete dust on the windowsills—it was a theme, like Cuban or Sports. He cut the voice off, got out, locked the door and made his way up the path to the last house on the road. The owners couldn't have foreseen that they would become frontier dwellers. A German shepherd stared out at him from the living-room window. After knocking, Gerald glanced back to make sure he'd attached the Community Patrol magnet to his car.

The man who answered the door leaned over a walking frame. 'One vehicle will drive up and park where you are there,' he gripped with one hand and pointed. 'And then another one will pull up behind it.' Gerald let him continue uninterrupted. 'It's not always obvious exactly what happens,' he said. 'Sometimes the driver of the first vehicle will get out and wander across there and then the next bloke will walk over to meet him, but on his way past he'll bend down somewhere in the vicinity of the other car's front wheel.' Gerald nodded. The man wasn't finished; he was just taking a breath. 'They don't say more than a few words to each other, then they turn back, get into their cars and drive away.'

Gerald waited a few moments to make sure the man had finished. He averted his gaze from the older man's shining pate. 'I see what you're saying. That doesn't seem right.' The German shepherd had appeared behind its owner and stood regarding Gerald—friend or foe, offender or defender, perpetrator or victim?

'The police told me to call if it happens again but what's the point? They'll be long gone. I asked if they wanted licence plate numbers and they weren't interested.'

'Well, I'll sit—'

'It was good enough for them to make all that noise in there doing their training exercises, before the houses came down.' He held the frame with one hand and waved towards the hundreds of lawns missing their houses. 'Running around in their outfits. Blowing things up. Spooked the dog.' The dog appeared to have recovered. Its gaze was steady. 'They said they'd done a mail drop beforehand but I never got anything.'

'I'll park myself over there for a while. Finish my coffee,' Gerald said. 'I might get out and wander along the river a little way.'

'You can if you like,' the old man said. 'Might put them off, I suppose.'

'They might decide it's not worth coming back,' Gerald said.

The man was already reversing in his walker. 'There are a lot of streets around here. How many cars have you got?'

The sun beat down and the temperature ramped up. Gerald tried sitting in the car with the windows open. He tried leaning on the bonnet nodding at passers by, most of whom had infants in pushchairs or dogs on leads. Many wore caps or sunhats with wide brims and he coveted their shade. He was soon drawn beyond the bollards to the cracked and disintegrating seal of the abandoned road, where the willows and eucalyptus provided enough shade for everyone. A blousy haze of green, a hush of stillness and light, lay over the snaking river. He looked downriver towards the beach at New Brighton, then upriver towards the city. A young woman in Lycra guided a buggy around the worst blisters in the seal. She had the high, bleached-blonde ponytail of a national hockey player or a nurse from a soap opera. He glanced at the supple push of her walking away. There was another track of bald dirt and dust directly beside the river, raised on a kind of dyke.

Gerald turned back to the street. No further cars had pulled in. He was about to retire for the day, to knock on the man's door and say goodbye, when the bright clothing of a young child caught his eye, about ten metres away on the track beside the river. A girl—she couldn't have been more than five or six—on a rise, out in the sun, nest of fair hair glowing. Then he couldn't see her. He could still hear her, though, or what seemed to be her—a blend of laughter and chatter.

There was actually a playground within sight, but that was on the other side of the river and cordoned off. The red tape was brighter than the faded primary colours of the swing set and slide. The giggle again. He couldn't tell where it was coming from. It was almost creepy against the backdrop of the deserted playground, the roads branching off into nothing, into more nothing, on the other side of the river, pointless kerbs and street signs.

He looked both ways, upriver and downriver, but couldn't see an adult. The track she'd been on dropped fairly smartly on the river side, he knew, into a morass of reeds and rushes, waist deep for a five-year-old, a challenge for little legs. He put his keys back in his pocket and walked in a casual mosey towards the spot where he'd last seen her. If he got to within five metres of her, that would be close enough to make a dash for it if he needed to. She could potter, oblivious, under his supervision, until someone came to claim her. He still couldn't see her—then suddenly he could. She was on the road only a few metres away. She met his look with wide, half-startled eyes. He stopped, smiled. He hadn't counted on interaction. From a distance she had seemed unkempt but her clothing was in fact quite fashionable, if that could be said of a child's clothes. She was more agile up close, more in command of herself than he might have expected. 'Hello,' he said. She didn't speak. She didn't potter. She stared. Then she opened her mouth and yelled back into the trees.

'Mum!' That was where the other sounds had come from: the shade of the trees, where a woman stood and scooped up a toddler.

It wouldn't even be his first confrontation that week. The previous weekend he had been returning with his wife from his son's house in Kaiapoi, driving along a stretch of road on the outskirts, beside the market gardens, past orchards and outfits selling motorcycle parts and cray pots, where the speed limit was higher, where a sign said:

> CANVAS
> FEED
> SADDLERY

Nobody had any business being out of their cars on the side of the road in the dark in a place like that, let alone scuffling with another person in the range of his headlights. He saw them up ahead on the side of the road, in time to slow down but not to stop. At the lesser speed he could make out a man and woman: he in torn jeans, she in not-a-lot (short skirt, bare arms). They noticed Gerald's car before he was all the way past. He saw quite clearly the man's reddened, angry eyes because they were pointed directly at his, taking their own measure.

'Don't get involved,' said Gerald's wife beside him. She needn't have bothered. He had long ago absorbed her opinions. She had no interest in outreach. She had always been more inclined to protect her own patch. 'Keep driving,' she said, but he couldn't ignore a woman in distress, regardless of who she chose to associate with. He couldn't live with that on his conscience.

He came to a stop fifty metres past them. He made sure the road ahead was clear, looked in his side mirror, checked his blind spot and pulled the car into a U-turn. He coasted nearer, and slowed to a stop. The engine and the windscreen were between him and the couple, if that was what they were. The man was holding the woman by the arm and when Gerald opened the car door he dropped it. The woman was breathing deeply, puffing even as she turned towards Gerald. Strings of tattoos ran up her thin limbs. They both had the red film over their eyes. The man squared up to Gerald. 'What the fuck do you want?' Gerald turned his body sideways, as he had been trained to do when faced with an aggressor.

'Fuck off!' The woman shouted, and straight away she was on him with clawing fingernails and then fists. He put his arms up and crabbed backwards. There was no time to ask her if she was all right.

'I'm sorry!' he said. 'I'm sorry, sorry.' He backed into the open car door, arms still held high. The woman left off her attack for a moment and was looking through the windscreen at his wife in the passenger seat. Gerald took the opportunity to duck behind the door. Later he would ask himself what he was apologising for, and who he was apologising to.

'Get in!' his wife said. He could hear the fear in her voice. Nothing good happened in murky drizzle at night on the berms of roads where the only houses were down long driveways and half-concealed by car bodies.

The woman hurled abuse at him from where she stood, but her words were washed with the headlights and engine noise from passing cars. Lives poured past them at speed. None slowed or stopped. The man stood still, watching.

When they'd gone, his anger would slide away from Gerald, back to her. Gerald sank sideways into his seat, keeping his eyes on the woman, her scrawl of dark hair and pale skin, until he had pulled the door closed. He pressed the lock button. He would never get through to them, that was clear.

'Go!' his wife said.

By the time he turned off his bedside light and pulled his sheets up to his chin, whatever it was that was going to happen would have happened.

On the corner of their street stood an unmarked memorial garden consisting of a lawn and a few shrubs. In the house that had been there, a man had killed his wife and another woman who came to the door—strangled them and buried them under the floorboards. The council had pulled it down after repeated arson attempts. Gerald had been disconcerted—frightened, even—by the apocalyptic glow he had seen from his window the night of the biggest fire. The next morning there was the charry smell and visible scorching of the house's weatherboard exterior. He didn't entirely disapprove of the arsonist's impulse, though. Fire might be what it took to ward off a bad business like that. A few years later, after each aftershock, he'd asked himself, *What's happened to those girls?* He thought of their bodies lying there, vulnerable, in what state he hated to think, with liquefaction bubbling up around them. For a few moments at least, his mind wouldn't allow reason in, wouldn't bestow him with the knowledge that of course those girls (women) had been taken away long before the earthquakes—buried properly and cried over. They were gone.

'What do you want?' The woman was glaring at him. She was an adult version of the little girl. In fact she was the woman he had seen earlier with the pushchair, the hockey player or nurse, neither or both. The toddler in the pushchair was a boy. His brow was already creasing at the tone in her voice.

I'm sorry. He was going to say it. Sorry, I'm sorry. He opened his mouth but something different came out instead. 'I thought she was going to fall in,' he said. It wiped the belligerent expression off her face. He turned and walked away. Everything was as it had been before. Green, still, hot. He hadn't attracted any attention.

When he encountered the two men loitering on the river side of the bollards—saying nothing much, doing nothing much—he gave them a nod. He used his electronic key to open the car. He did notice the two cars parked outside the last house in the row, but if he called it in, what would he even say? There are two cars parked outside a house. There are two men standing beside a river.

DIANA BRIDGE

Accommodations

for Swan

I.

She has walked through the Gardens to the camellias,
to where tiers of steps part the glossy bushes
and she is encircled by leaves. It is the same
and always different. Above her, a white magnolia;
each year it throws up, with its tide of flowers,
some distinctive conceit. She is thinking
of me—we were children encircled
by stories. It is too cold to meet.

A voice has cancelled the blaze. The magnolia
lifts emptied branches to colourless sky.
It has held back its crop—just a few tight buds,
then it wavered. A connection has thinned
and failed. She doesn't know why. The hill
to her right links suburbs like sections of spine.
The tree, as the crow flies, is equidistant
between her house and mine.

2

I stand in the place where she stood
and conjured likeness. On a grid of limbs
which the sun has edged with navy, a flock
of white unfolding bodies, smooth ovoids
that have settled there like birds. Wings
down, chests up, or is it throats extended—
what is it they extol? Here's passion
enough to reinvent the whole tradition.

Come on, John Donne, come Hopkins—
what, this year, do they bring?
A splash of camellia, crimson in a corner
of a print; a refined asymmetry that must be
Japanese. An enduring play of pattern
and, threading the air, the lovely
accommodations of friendship,
the stabbing start of spring.

ROWAN TAIGEL

Mothers & Fathers

we lay on the bed facing
each other like grown-ups after
he rolled off me sending

eddies of dust motes upward
we felt beyond our years
sepia beams from the little window catching

the overturned apple crate for a table,
dented metal teapot and china teacup,
with its cracked, grey lifeline

as we'd rehearsed, I'd put the baby to bed
he'd tell me about his day at work
I'd bring him cups of tea

in the abandoned shed we'd claimed for a hut
then I'd lie down on my back and wait
to feel his body fill my hollows like concrete

he'd kiss me, move his tongue around
the way French people do, soft, insistent probing
the newspaper stuffed in the crack between

wall and ceiling, pale, like the underside of an arm
air pressed from my lungs, he lay on top
of me on the mattress beside

the mauve satin curtain I'd sometimes pull
away from the window and tuck around myself
like a tent, the inside of a hot-air balloon,

a parachute before catching a fall.

OWEN BULLOCK

One Letter

One perfect letter rolls through the pages
offering the balancing art of spheres
ousting the fragment and the broken line
opening outwards to enclose us all
or turning inwards to contemplate self.
Onions resemble and start out that way.
Orators begin and end on a theme.
Opera the vowel, let it unsing sense—
options never end, the infinite
ornaments take over space in cycles
outering ripples to the lake's far edge
organising bubbles, droplets, seeds, fruits
ordering pebbles on disordered shores
once the moon has crept into hurdled light
over the horizon past the hours at
odds with the stationary lines we built
our vacuum-packed safety, harbouring us
operating day & night through tired storms
oblivious to daily patterning—
oil fosters all manner of devices
otherwise too simple, like a new egg ...
Oops! The hand lets slip, a mistake, or an
opportunity, things to evolve, what
other choice do we have, how to see, what
outfits to sew with words & sequins, how
often appreciate our first last world
ourselves called within it by cooing birds—
ooh the colour of slow curved horizon.

MURRAY EDMOND

Selfie

Alan noticed his face was coming apart. The lower section was slipping. The upper was rising. The immediate effect produced was of sad surprise, but the long-term prognosis promised a deep fissure, a parting of ways, a painful separation from himself. He called his best friend, Allen. There was only a message: 'Allen is not available. Leave him a message.' 'Allen, this is Alan, I need to speak to you. Call me. If you call after one, I shall be driving, until two, so won't be able to answer.'

He had to make a delivery thirty kilometres to South Auckland, on the edge of town, where the pine trees mingled with parking lots and storage units. Someone needed one of his rechargers for their battery-powered water heating. He was having to do his own deliveries this week because Alana had taken annual leave. Alana had always wanted to visit Alcatraz. She was setting out to write a history of the prison and this would be her first visit. Alan had agreed he could cover the deliveries this week. Business was almost at a halt anyway. The weeks after Christmas were when batteries were running down, but no had woken up to the fact yet. Come the end of January it would all pick up. Alana had chosen a good time to be away.

When he got there, no one was at the house. He tried the number he had been given. No answer. Alan sat in the car reading his favourite book, *Aslan the Lion: A study in metempsychotic psychology*. Alan belonged to the Autist Society (nothing to do with autism). Autists believed that somewhere in the world, given the billions and billions of people and the natural limitations on genetic permutations, there must be someone who was exactly the same as them. The aim of the Autist Societies, which were scattered across the globe and maintained a deliberately low profile, was to find ways and means whereby these identical pairings of selves, once discovered, could merge, so that consciousness might be transferred back and forth and one would no longer be confined by the body one was born with. The Autists were seeking the psychological equivalent of the battery rechargers that Alan spent large parts of his mortal existence marketing, and one of which now lay on the back seat of his worn-out Audi.

Chapter Three: 'Aslan's Answer'. Alan put his finger on the first sentence and gazed out the window. At the top of a tall macrocarpa an awkward-looking bird, large and clumsy, was struggling to maintain its balance on the supple branches. The bird, which looked like a cross between a pelican and eagle—well, yes, rather like an auk—suddenly slipped and Alan saw it fall, down the macrocarpa's slippery greenery. Alan's head wormed out through the open window in time to see the auk, if that was what it was, hit the sea of grey pebbles with a muffled thud and an angry squawk.

Alan found he was staring straight into his side-mirror. His lips were turning into jowls, his jaw had thickened and hung like a heavy avocado. His eyebrows had lifted and a dome of wrinkles formed across his forehead. His phone went off: *a-aaa, a-aaa, a-aaa*. It was Allen. He laid the phone to his ear: 'Alan!' Allen was not the double Alan was seeking, but for a while each of them had thought they had found their same other.

'Can I call at your house on the way home, Allen?'

'Sorry, Alan, I'm away. Alas, I'm up north till after Anzac Day.'

'I need someone to look at me and tell me what they think.'

'Always happy to take a look at you, Alan. Probably a case of …' and then the line went awry.

Alan shook the phone. 'Allen! Allen!' No answer. What had Allen said? Alan felt he had almost caught the word. Amalgamation? Was that it? He could put out a post on the Autists' site on the dark web asking for answers. That always invited alarmists but it would be worth it. He would do it tonight. Alan gripped his own arm. At the rate his face was changing, would he even make it to tonight?

He picked out one almond from the little bag he kept on the passenger seat: arrgh, stale as. His phone *a-aaa*-ed again. It was only a text—Alana letting him know how it was all going: 'Amazing.' That was it. Alan annulled the text. He held his phone up in front of his face and took a photo. He didn't look as bad as he had in the side-mirror—more like his old self. Perhaps the change had begun to reverse itself. Quickly he glanced in the side-mirror again, but it was not good. This time it announced a different story. How could that be? A scrambling and a shuffling and a grunting interrupted Alan's anxiety. The auk was crawling with its wings across the bonnet of the Audi, dragging a line of blood after it, an after-image of Hitchcock's film. It slithered up the windscreen and disappeared onto the roof.

Something tapped at the roof of the car just above his head. Alan's heart accelerated. Was the auk about to attack?

'Sorry, sir, sorry!' Suddenly there were two faces peering in at him through the open window. Smiling faces. Asian faces. 'It's us,' the faces said in concert. 'Arthur and Ann—for the batteries.' Alan sensed he must appear alarmed. 'We didn't mean to ambush you.'

'Anguish me—no, no, you didn't anguish me.' What a strange expression to use.

'Ambush. Ambush!' Ann almost shrieked the word as she laughed.

'Ah,' said Alan, 'got it!' Arthur was also laughing. 'Let me get out of the car.' Arthur and Ann backed away as Alan emerged. 'Good, you've arrived. What did you say your names were?'

'I'm Ann and this is Arthur—Abish. Abish is our name.' They looked at Alan's face as if they knew why it looked as it did. Hangdog. 'We're Jews, Chinese Jews. Our families came from Kaifeng.'

Alan's eyebrows rose, his forehead seemed to smile, his head nodded. Were they kidding?

'You looked rather aghast for a moment there,' Arthur added.

'Just thinking,' said Alan.

'No, before—when we arrived and gave you a fright.' Alan looked at Ann and wished Alana was here. Then his eyes flicked across the car (what would they think of the blood?), inspecting the roof, trying to find signs of the auk's passage up the bonnet, over the windscreen ... and where had it gone? He scanned the carpark. There was nothing to see, nothing to be seen.

'Shall we?' asked Ann. 'Sorry we're late; the fact is we're in rather a hurry.' Who was it she reminded Alan of? That woman in that film his father used to watch on his pirated VHS tapes—what was it called? Some vision of the future ... *Alphaville*. Ann looked like the actress from *Alphaville*. Amie? Anna? Anouk?

'Is this it?' asked Arthur, who had spotted the battery recharger on the back seat and was already opening the door and lifting it out.

'It's heavy,' said Alan.

'No problem; I'm an angioplastist,' Arthur assured him.

Ann laughed. 'I'm sure the poor man doesn't know what that is.' Then, to Alan, 'How much do we owe you?' Alan found the invoice on his phone and held it up while Ann swiped her card. 'All done.'

'Tell me,' Alan called after them as they headed down an alleyway towards their house, with the large recharger tucked under Arthur's arm. Ann and Arthur both turned. 'Tell me ... how do you ... I ... how do you think I look?'

'Look?'

'Ah, yes, how do I look?'

'You look anguished!' roared Ann and they all began to laugh.

'Maybe it's you who needs the recharger!' said Arthur. 'Plug it into your amygdala.'

'Don't drop it,' Alan called.

'Snug as a bug!' Arthur called back, and they were gone, around the corner of the tin fence where the alley began.

Alan's arm ached. He shook it like a damp towel. The pain shot into the other arm. Ah! He flapped both his arms. Amygdala. He'd heard that word. What was it? He racked his brain but nothing came. Ah well, another day.

As he turned back towards the Audi he saw immediately that someone was in his car. What the ...? Of course he hadn't locked it, not to cross the carpark. Someone—something—was sitting in the driver's seat staring out. Alan approached apprehensively. When the occupant came into focus he saw the auk sitting there, its wings resting on the steering wheel. Alan's amazement did not preclude an autonomic reaction. Thrusting his cellphone before him he had the presence of mind to archive the image. He'd send it tonight to the Autists. And to Allen and Alana.

Something amazing had happened to him. At last. Shaking, he opened the image on the phone. Well, clearly he had been shaking as well when he took the shot. He zoomed in. The image advanced and, as it did, the pixels accumulated. But there was no doubting who sat there. He knew, when he looked back up, that the car would be void of avian animation.

WES LEE

And I Suppose Poems Could Be Miniature Rooms (each time you begin with the hope of creation)

After 'The Rape Kit's Secret History' by Pagan Kennedy, *New York Times*

for Marty Goddard

I do remember the peace I had once
going back home to visit,
sitting in the chair I always sat in, and everything moved
as it should in the vale of peace where time had stopped.
And there was a low-key feeling of pleasure in my body.
And the sadness of realisation: *Why couldn't it always be like this?*

And this realisation happened at the time,
not after when I had left,
which is usually the case.
A strange long moment like
billions of years of time compressed.
Like a river that wobbles and seems to stop moving in the same direction.

The moment was like a door in a doll's house opened
and a light shining out,
and all the other doors open to dark rooms where things happened,
where things are still happening.

And I read about a woman activist
who made miniature rooms in the evenings:
dioramas portraying a mother and children;
each room lit with a tiny lampshade.
Until her whole apartment was filled.

The woman activist invented the rape kit.
A cardboard box containing a pencil, a comb, a forensic list, swabs
and slides.
It was said she became a 'furious alcoholic'.
She alienated friends and family in the last months of her life.
It was said she withdrew, surrounded by the miniature model rooms
she loved to build.
It was said she vanished, shrinking down to nothing.
It was said she asked that her ashes be thrown to the winds
in Sedona, Arizona, along the red cliffs.
Old friends didn't even know she was gone.

But the rape kit survives.

And I think of the untested rape kits, abandoned,
warehoused, eaten by rats, mouldering under leaky ceilings.
Thousands upon thousands of minutes of pain,
of unimaginable terror
left to waste.

And the rooms she made with leadlight windows and painted French doors;
a lily pond;
a faraway gaze.
These perfect oases of domesticity,
everything calm.

CHRIS PRICE

Marsyas Becoming Parchment

The work of making parchment is unglamorous,
and sometimes it smells like the inside of a boxing glove
—Mary Wellesley

Now what to make
of the skinbag, the bonesack?
We all agreed we didn't need
another wineskin. Some wanted him
strung up in the forum
as a billboard for insults,
rage and warnings
of future pain, but first

we needed to revise him.
While it still held the whiff
of the locker room
we soaked his shaggy hide
in lime and slung it
over the stump to strip
the nap from its follicles
with the scudder's blade

and uncover the faint blueprint
of river-veins within.
Already pliant, the skin would take
the contours of whatever
it was draped on, and as some of us
were mothers, after all,
we pressed it briefly to our cheeks
reviewed the baby face

it still contained, then stretched
him on the herse, tied him
with string and twisted the pegs
till he looked like a drumskin
and we recalled the tap
of his hooves as he danced,
those nights when he had his pick
of the most pleasing among us

the ones who needed a lift
or a favour, or who, by night's end,
he'd simply backed into a corner.
We poured the scalding water on
like washerwomen, stripped
what was left of the fat
with the crescent luna, then again,
again, until all visible trace

was gone and we could hang him out
to dry in the oven room where
the smell was ever so slightly
soured milk. We took him out warm
for the loving last attentions
of the blade that brings
both pleasure and pain:
if you get the angle right,

the steel will croon ice-
music (Persephone calling
through a distant fissure
from the place where the god
still holds her captive). Then
he was ready to be trimmed.
We used the offcuts to repair
some ancient and neglected texts

but for the rest, chose private
reckoning: a book bound in
a thicker, tougher square of him
where we each had a page
smooth as a milk-tooth to fill
as we wished—all words and deeds
by which the world had known him
dispelled, erased, made clean.

PETER BELTON

Ralph Hotere Finds his Balance

Beyond the fire and the rain are
the bones of recollection to be found in
sands and strands where the kuaka awaits
the call to flight. Straight lines through and across
the light of time measured in seasons and a reaching
into the sump of night. The blackness of it is penetrated only
by the trajected spike of flight which the eye must follow, so.
And as season follows season, Ralph Hotere must restore
balance in his cosmos through the awaited play of
reflection with the tricks of inversion and return
where patterns might be discovered upon the
skin of this black pond inside which the
mirror of thought and a polishing
of his gaze delivers.

MICHAEL HARLOW

Strange Times

My son says his head hurts. He points to the spot
just below his heart. At the window, he is counting
trees that he has never climbed. And the birds he
loves and wants to whistle hello to. I can hear him
talking to the animals flying through the air, a confetti
of wings, and then disappearing.

He wants to know where they fly to when they
take off like that. A curtain of hard rain is falling.
His head rocking from side to side. What's the use,
he says, I think I am always going to hear those wild
dogs barking in the night.

EWAN McDOUGALL

Painting Animal

1. *Ahoy!*, 2020, oil on canvas, 1200 x 1500mm
2. *Man Seeing The Light*, 2020, oil on canvas, 1200 x 1500mm
3. *Doin' Lines*, 2020, oil on canvas, 1200 x 1500mm
4. *Sunrise: Nebuchadnezzar*, 2018, oil on canvas, 1223 x 910mm
5. *Bonzer Cracker Shag*, 2020, Triptych: oil on canvas, 1223 x 2730mm
6. *Bloody Oath!*, 2020, Diptych: oil on canvas, 1223 x 1820mm
7. *Level WTF*, 2020, oil on canvas, 760 x 760mm
8. *Man with Wild Ideas*, 2020, oil on wood and frame, 650 x 550mm

Painting for me is life itself. As a young man I lived, loved and hated the 'party animal' life.

Now I am a painting animal and have been for thirty-two years. My influences are the Māori rock art in the caves of Kurow; the impossibly ancient pictographs of the Kakadu Aboriginal people; the work of modern painters such as Picasso, Nolde, Appel, Dubuffet, Boyd, Ken Kiff, Peter Cleverley and Philip Clairmont; and the imprinted careening drunk, drugged up, hair on end, desperately hanging on to the perpetual party.

I prize spontaneity, vibrant colour, wild figures cavorting and leering in ecstasy or howling in pain but somehow making it through the cacophony.

I work every day, unless overseas or travelling for an exhibition or holiday.

It is work but it is no grind; it is exhilarating and fulfilling; it is to lose the self and yet, happily, to be found.—Ewan McDougall

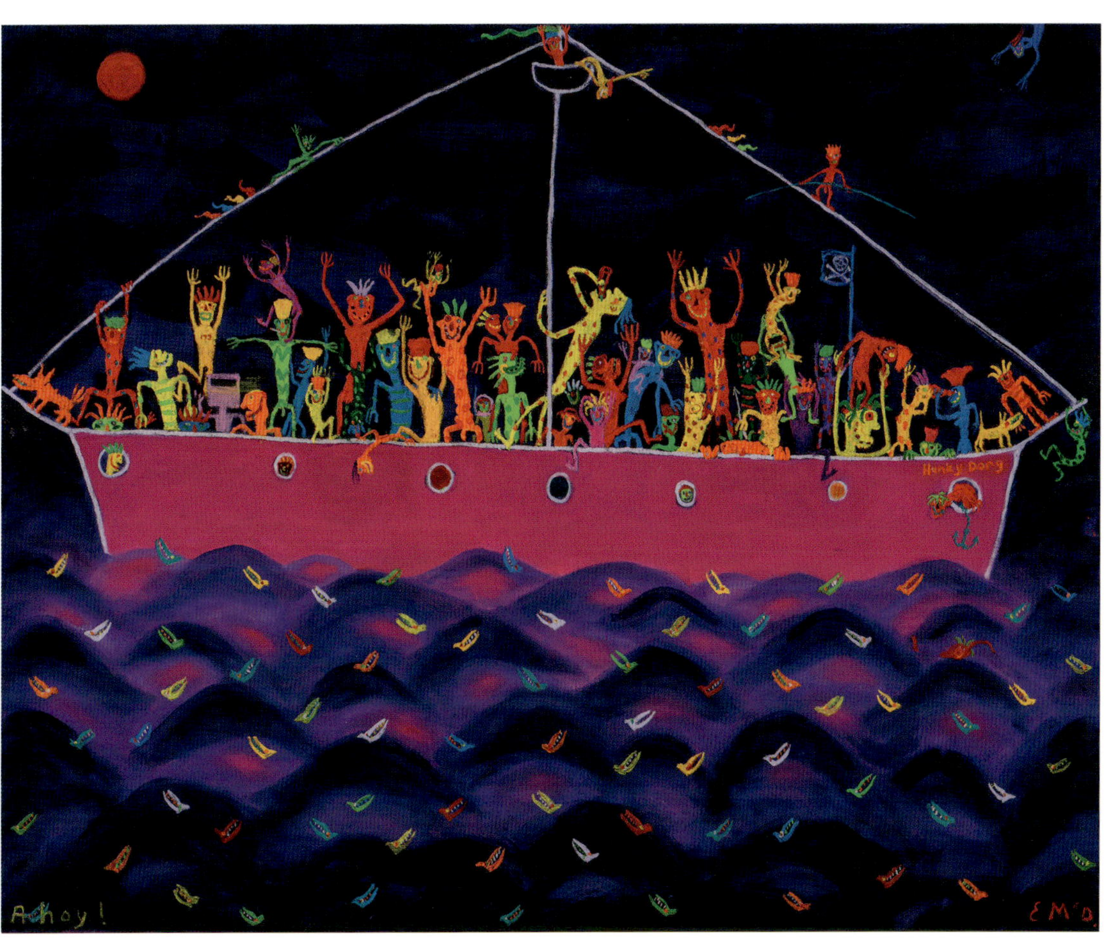

Ahoy!
E McD.

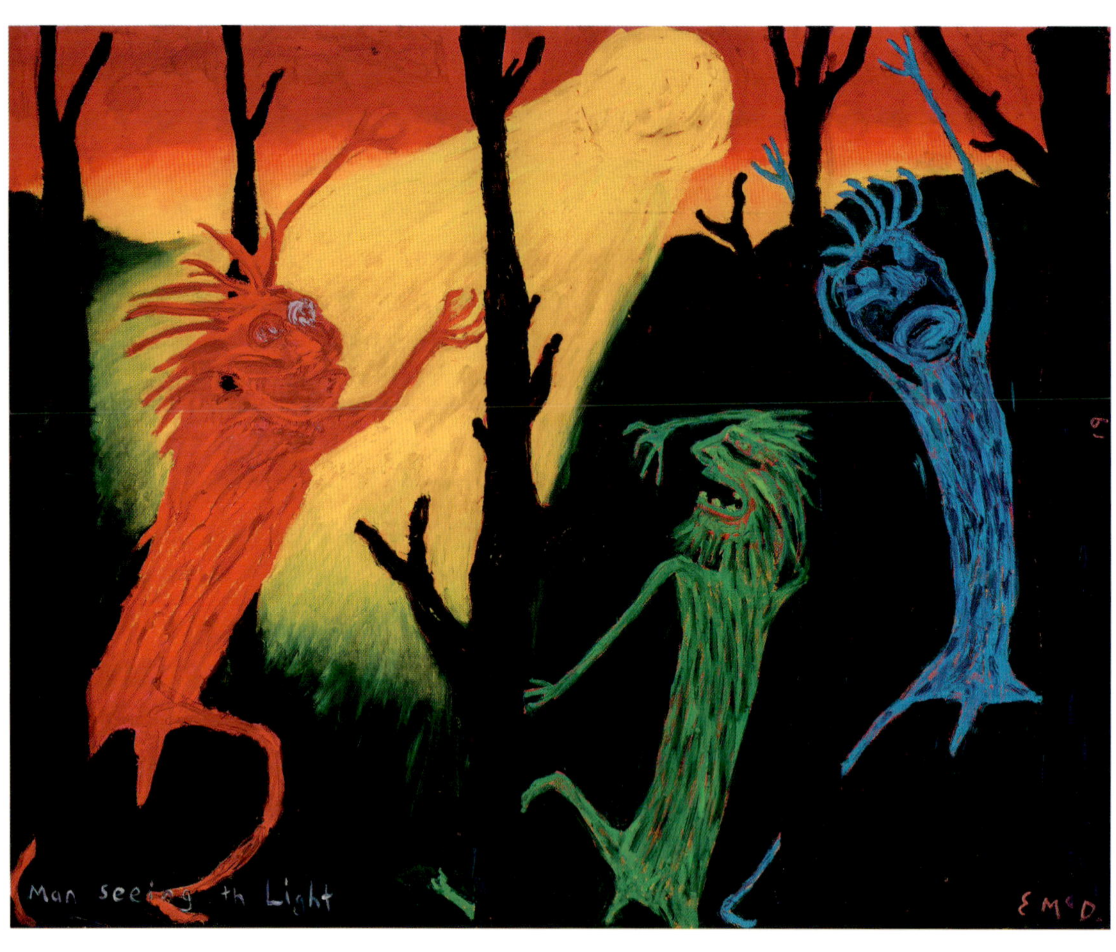
Man seeing th Light
E McD.

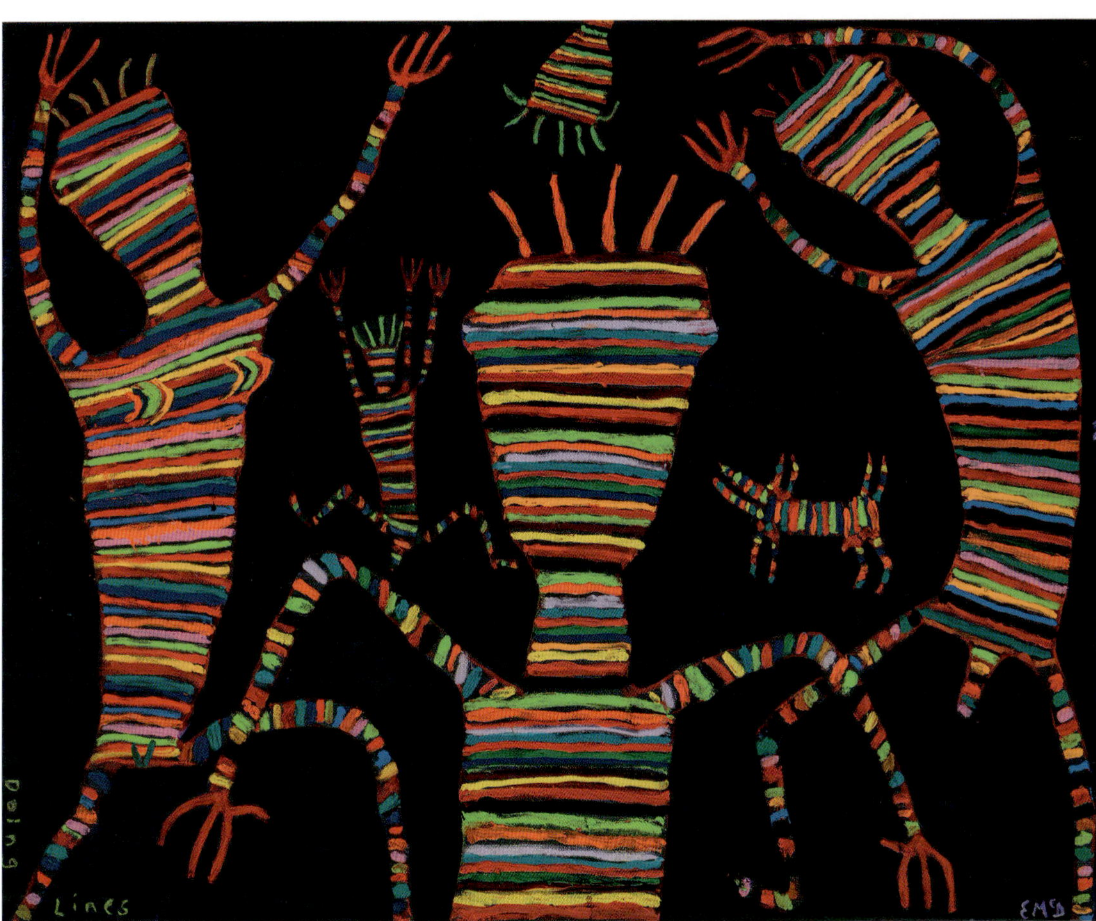
Doing
Lines
EMcD

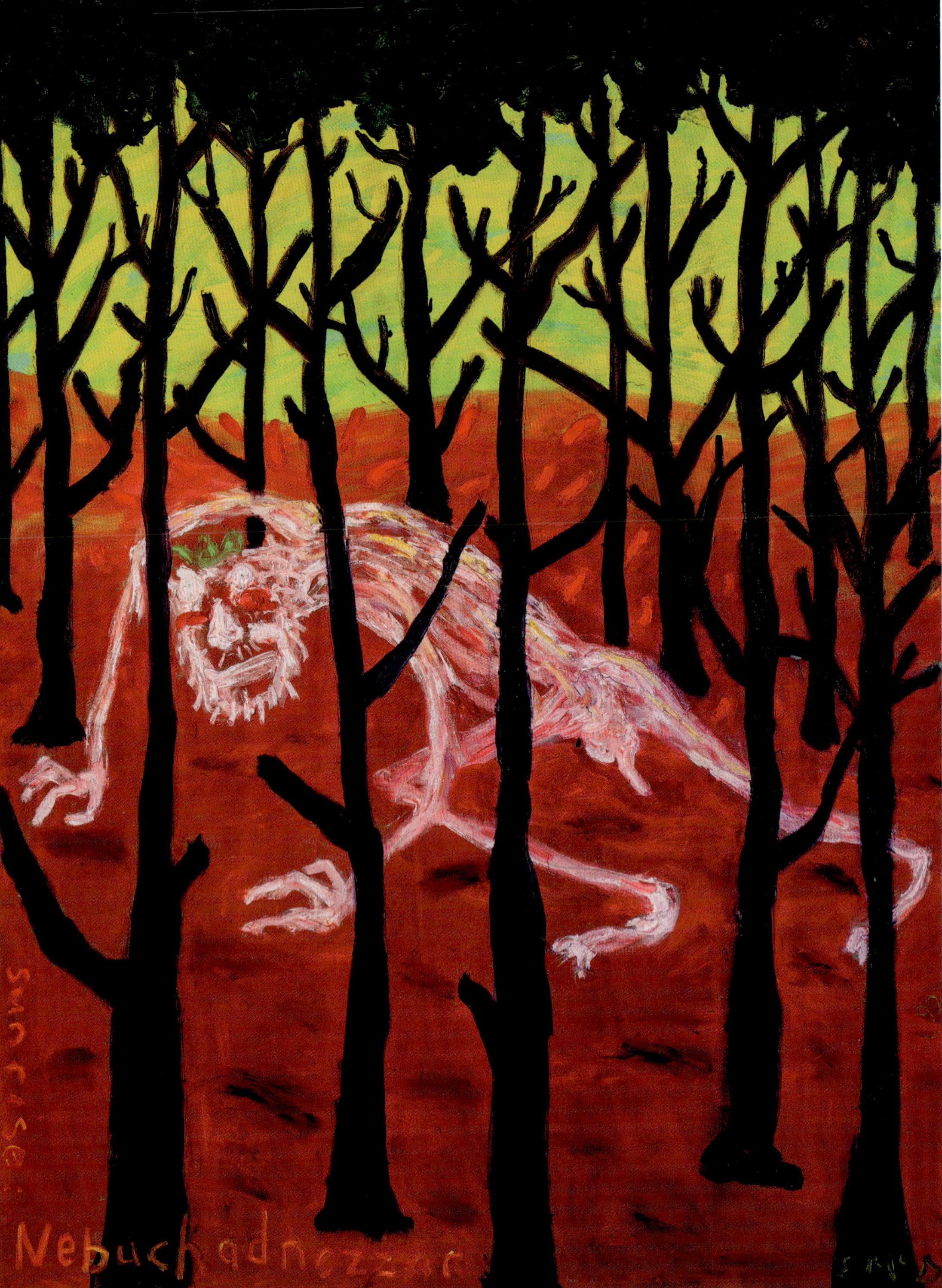
sunrise:
Nebuchadnezzar

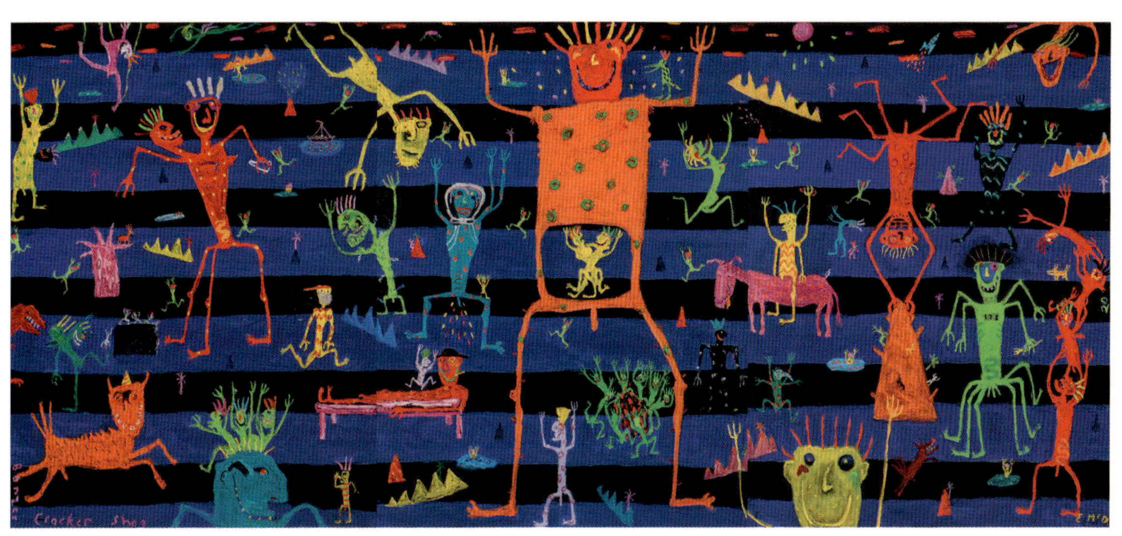

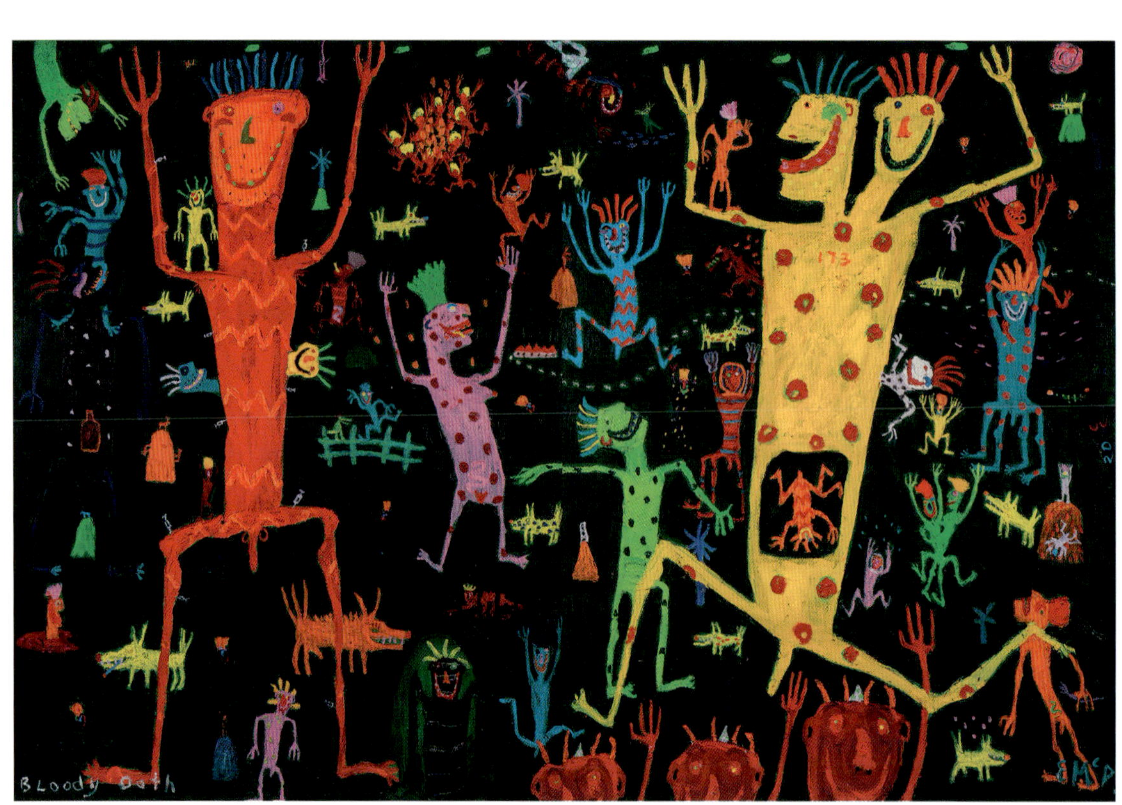
BLoody Oath

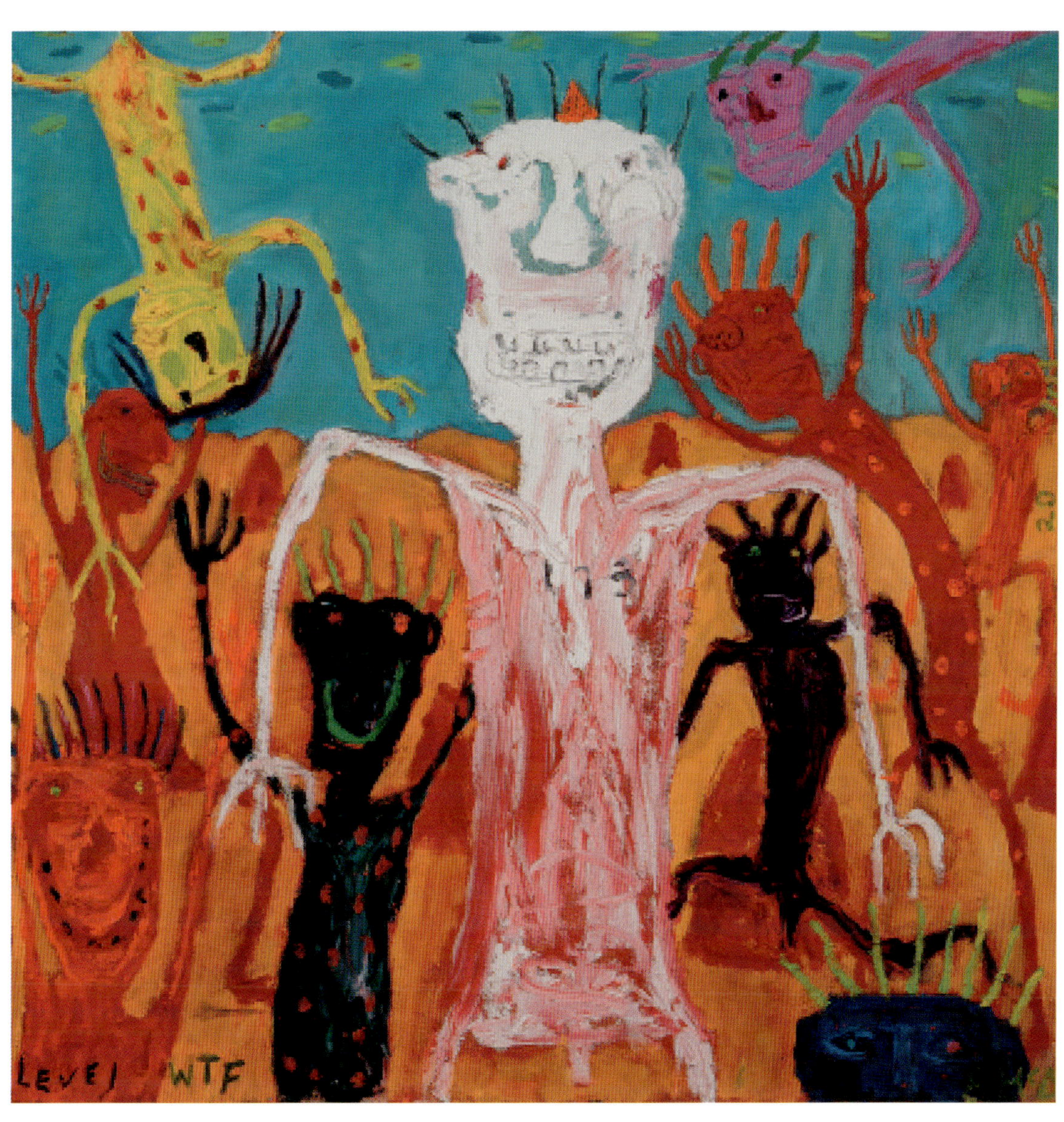
LEVEL WTF

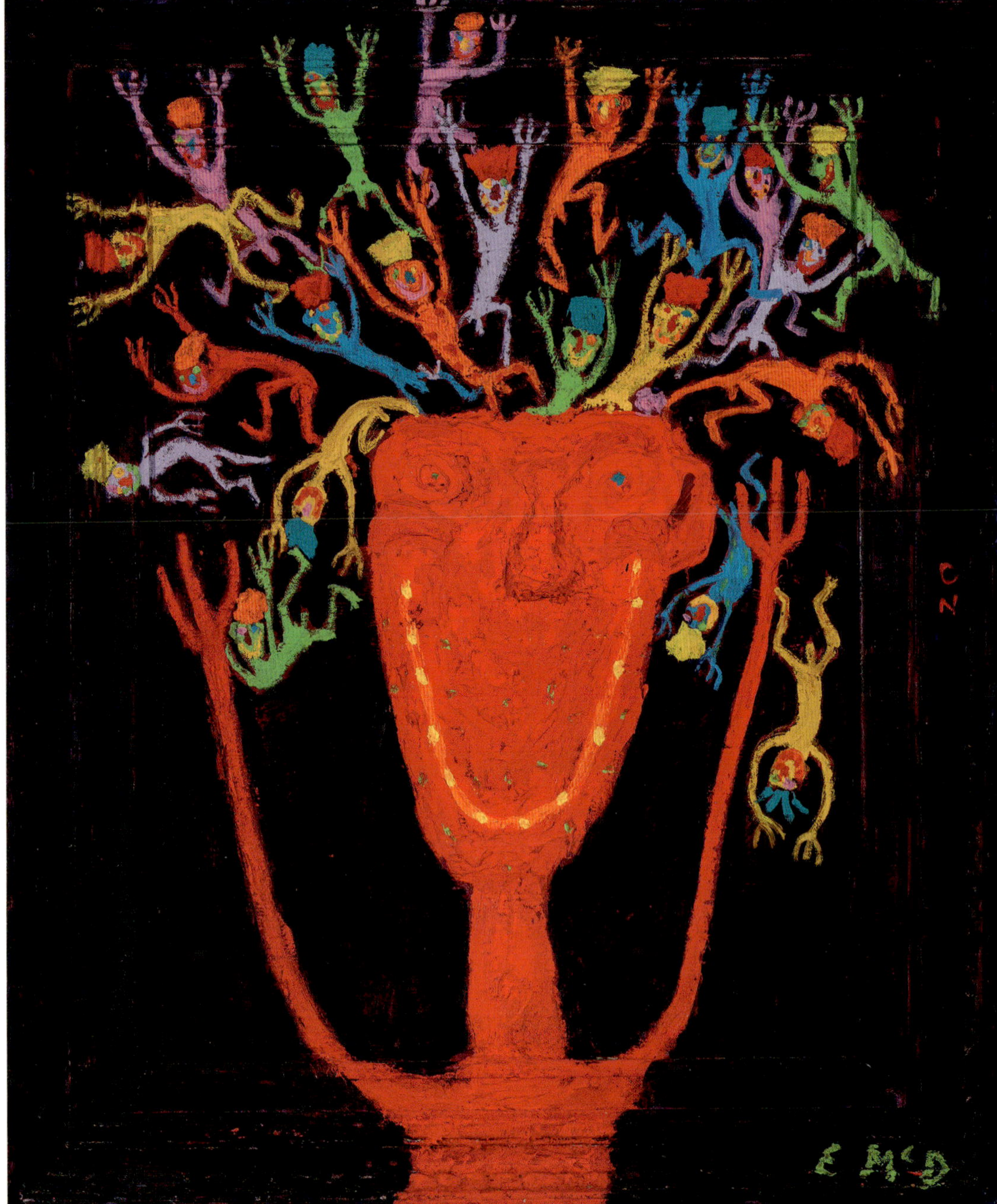
E McD

SARAH LAWRENCE

The Best Day

My Best Day had its wings clipped. I forget it often, like the darkwood floor under old carpet, that cool edge to the sink of a footstep. Postal address: Yellowed Grassfields, Samford Valley, Brisbane, Australia; that is to say, everywhere. That thick steam heat that sticks to your skin. It feels like childhood to me.

When I was three I owned the paddocks, and the ant-traps, and the eucalyptus trees, up high in the sky where the sugar-gliders swing. I would run with imaginary antelope packs, pricking my feet with burrweed, spreading seeds in my wild hair, hurtling down gravel paths on tricycles, having no secrets, and I was in love. I was in love.

My first love was the world, all of it, though children do not know what Love is. I loved the world before I knew to cut my love in pieces. I loved before I discovered the sad fact that one cannot love everything, not really, and I loved with a savagery I have yet to replicate. But most of all, I loved the chickens.

There were four of them, my hens, the colour of burnt toast, with deep red wattle crowns and glass button eyes. They lived in a castle pen across a drawbridge, behind a tall wire fence to keep the nightfoxes out: Sally, Ginger, Georgia and Kiev. I fed them every morning before sunrise, when the air was golden and dewy. They would chirp their hellos, I would sing my good-days, and when I was close, they would kneel beside me so I could pull them up into my chubby arms. On the best mornings, they would fill my palms with four speckled eggs.

Their feed was of thin cylindrical pellets, which they plucked from my fingers as if they were precious stones. I always wondered what transpired inside the little planets of the hens' pea-sized heads. Perhaps those pellets, which to me smelled purely of brownmulch, to them twinkled and glittered in ways I could never conceive. I liked to believe they did; I liked to believe that everything was beautiful to something. We kept the glittering pellets in a sealed black box, free from orange nostrils and curious beaks. Too much of a beautiful thing and a hen can eat herself to death, growing so big so quickly that her heart cannot keep time.

One particular midsummer morning, with the sun peeping and jangling against the grassflints, I skipped my footsteps, springing chimebells, across the lake of The Best Day. I knew that day would be The Best Day, the way you sometimes know things inside your bones. When someone walks across your grave, they say you shiver.

My footsteps took me, as they always did, down that path to my four hens. I can see them still, huddled by their stiff door, waiting for me, their feathers in every shade of russet, the brittle plasticine quills from which sprouted the down; if you looked closely enough, their eyes were black Saturns with rings of brilliant amber. A morning trapped in resin. I stroked their heads with my fingertips. They pecked the ruffles of my skirts. Back then, I could speak every language.

Five little monkeys, sitting in a tree
Teasing Mr Crocodile, 'You can't catch me!'
Along came Mr Crocodile
Quiet as can be ...

I sang to my hens as I opened their favourite black box, and they gathered at my feet. Eight Saturns orbiting the singing Sun. I do not remember how it felt to be young and to not know it, but I remember the warmth of The Best Day beating at my back, I remember the brush of the hens and the words of the songs. I was so in love, so in love, so in love that the words drummed like a heartbeat, so in love that my love was everything between the earth and the clean sphere stretch of the sky; I do not remember the love. I stood, in love, and suddenly the soil was I, and the leaves were I, and the creek beneath the drawbridge was I, the winds were I, the chickens and the eggs were I, I, I, I, and I saw the pellets glitter. I saw them twinkling in the sun, and I felt how my hens loved them, because I loved everything, and it was The Best Day, and I had the most wonderful idea.

I wanted to share The Best Day. I wanted to break off pieces of it and throw them at the world.

I looked down at the box of beautiful pellets, those jewels flickering in the light, and I thought how selfish I had been to lock them each morning from the chickens who loved them so. To think that, day after day, I had taken their speckled eggs back up the path to eat in luxury, and all the while they waited, helpless, for the next sunrise in my imposed moderation. How beautiful it would be to give my hens everything, just for one day. The Best Day.

One by one, I lifted each beloved bird from the ground, up, up, into that forbidden black box. I watched them cluck and rustle with glee, and happy tears pricked my eyes to see the joy I had fashioned, fashioned from thin air.

Four little monkeys, sitting in a tree
Teasing Mr Crocodile, 'You can't catch me!'
Along came Mr Crocodile
Quiet as can be ...

I sang once more, to calm my hens. They nestled into their feast like kingly dragons over a hoard. When I saw the eight blinking Saturns sleepy and shut, I placed the black lid over them and sealed it: a shield from the hot midday sun I knew was only hours away. A morning trapped in resin. I had given them love and songs and pellets. I had given them The Best Day.

That is how I left the chickens, sleeping in shade, bathing in riches as I traced my footsteps back up the path, hands cradling four speckled eggs. I imagined the sky smiling down at it all, this beautiful symbiosis I made.

In late afternoon my mother walked through the doorway with a look on her face that made the heat stick in my throat. I never coughed it clean. Somehow, I knew what she would say before she said it. I think I had always known.

For a while it remained the great mystery of our household, how those hens had found their way inside the feedbox, how they sealed it so well they asphyxiated on their own hellos. Must've been wily things. A hen can eat herself to death.

I did not tell a soul. To the world I was silent, so silent I forgot the love, I even forgot the truth. Love had made the pellets glittering bullets; Love had left the black air ringing with songs about monkeys and crocodiles; Love melted wings like son Icarus in the sun. There were things in the world I could not love. I made their bed good. I was three years old, and that was The Best Day. Every day after was a just little bit crooked.

That night we stood, mother and father and sister and murderer, blank-faced by the four corpses in that black box. We planted them in the earth, as if they might grow. As if speckled eggs might show up in the potato crop. When no one was watching, I clipped four hen-sized holes in my stainless love, let them wilt in that sickly heat. I bled a little, as all amputees do. I did not cry. As for the clippings, they're buried under eucalyptus, yellowed and festering like old smokers' teeth. An unmarked grave in the Samford hills.

My mother tells me that one morning before sunrise, when I was ten years old, I came downstairs to breakfast and calmly told her that seven years earlier I had killed Sally, Ginger, Georgia and Kiev. I had sung them to sleep, and they had died. I pulled the guilt from my backpack and left for school, finally free.

ERIK KENNEDY

Grief Sonnet 1 of 235

There's something nameless at the centre of
a grief, like a hiker seen through binoculars
who could be an electrician called Augustus
or a debt-haunted artist called Zuzanna,
and the more you look at the grief, which for
our purposes is a distant, blurry walker,
the more you transfer your distinct ideas
to the figure processing alone across
the darkening upland to a nearish carpark
or to a village of familiar companions
and adversaries who make up the fully
realised inner world of the namelessness.
All you can bring to this are your roadside guesses.
Is it really so unknowable? That sound you hear is yesses.

JOANNA AITCHISON

Miss Dust in a Motel Room

'There's Miss Dust,' says the door,
'trailing bitumen.' She's stumbling into

finding out. She's walking around
the room on stilts, picking her way

across the bodies stitched into the carpet.
Shrunken people are moving their mouths

inside the television. The enormous fluffy
microphone nods its *yes, yes* head.

Her brain spins like a bird in a cartoon.
Ambulance tunes, ambulance tunes.

JOANNA PRESTON

Galanthus in Rain

Soft rain bends the necks of winter flowers—
penitents in white veils and green blouses,
meek beneath the copper beech that towers
like a magistrate. And all my powers
of persuasion cannot alter how this
grim gallows-verdict falls: you are now hers.
Shapeless as salt water, thirty hours
since you left. Who knew we were such cowards?
—good wine left aside until it sours.
The house fills with rain. And I allow this.

CHRIS HOLDAWAY

from Parihaka/Pātaka Kai

In Ōkato where my friends live in a garage
There is a pātaka kai—being a shelf on the side
Of the town hall where food is exchanged—so
Abundant my shame turns to an invasive weed
I learn in fact has many uses. O informal
Nature. I come from a declaration of war; most
Fanatical complacency's absent-minded holocaust.
Stroke of business. Judgement of rot. Commit
To gardens instead and the absolute end of excess
By communal harvest. Where light itself off the
Angled blade of the mountain chops wood.
Through the smoke of creation anything can
Suddenly form the foundation of the whole
World: op-shop LP of themes from B-grade
Spy thrillers; selected 20th-century short stories
In a basket by the toilet; catalogue of a state house
Meticulously disassembled after an earthquake;
A definitive list of the nation's 4WD trails;
Whatever it is the digger driver reads on his
Phone unable to work for rain. Each grain a
Total solar eclipse; a small-town sports club
Enough to make me wonder what I'm doing
With my life. Cathedrals of factories and mines
The world over—and I have seen people give
Their entire lives for a corner store.

JOY TONG

Diaphony in C Minor

Inspired by the song 'Moon River'

I am lying belly up in the weeds
under Grafton Bridge, empty
as unheld hands.
Through phone speakers, Audrey's *dream-maker*
creaks among the pigeon coos

and the arches of my feet
remember their childlike ballet,
just for a moment, across the cemetery,
fresh dirt, tombstones. The clatter
of Symonds Street blurred
by grounded daydreams, the air
is Chopin études and *huckleberry friends*

yet ex-pianist fingers glissando
over pencilled biology notes
not the eighty-eight in black and white,
vocal cords hang untuned,
brain no longer wired
with film scores, instead memorising
the nervous system, each synapse
sparking from keys played, the pattern of inner ear
trembling like violin horsehair.

There is still sheet music buried beneath my bed
for the day I wake and listen, entranced again.
Till then I haunt recitals at St Matthew's,

dissolving in each slow chord,
and emerging, drifter, under-breath singer,
shy and crystallised and insatiable.

TIM SAUNDERS

Devoir

My great-great-grandfather
built a woolshed
out of tall trees
and pieces of birdsong
he found scattered in clearings.

Sometimes I still hear
a spectral choir
in that quiet time
after shearing,
an evening chorus
ensnared in axe-hewn walls.

My father took over
the family farm
when he left school.
I watched him tonight
listen to the old dog howl
at the moon trapped
in a frozen water bowl.

'I know how you feel,' he said.

I still don't know if he was talking to the dog
or the moon.

DAVID BEACH

Sixty 1

Sixty times I have kicked the earth around
the sun. Gravity isn't getting any
easier. I've still retained a bit of
magic in these toes though. Did you notice
how I negotiated the perihelion
back there? Well it was good, I assure
you. Keep in mind that I'm also looking
after the earth's spin. And the moon, that's
me too. I'm a regular circus
performer. But it's going to happen. By
which I suppose I mean it's going to happen
sooner rather than later. There will be
that tiny loss of balance and the next
thing I'll be giving the sun a header.

Sixty 8

Sixty-one in a couple of weeks. There's
a sense of having been tricked (you were
one of the angels, now all the other
angels are behind a cloud laughing at
you). This is what happens if you're gullible
enough to be born. I've been walking Te
Aro's plague streets. It's a bit like I
didn't make it to sixty-one. Straying
from our apartments or tombs the few
of us out and about flit silently
along, wearing a mask or else faces
a mask. We all wear four-metre-diameter
halo hoops, veering virtuously to
avoid socially distant collisions.

STEPHANIE BURT

Kite Day, New Brighton

Powdered sugar and cinnamon
under our toes and heels,
the seagulls seek expensive meals,
and the shallowest wash, in the heat of the day, still feels
too cold for wading. It conceals what it conceals.

The colour of soap on scuffed slate,
the beach can't rinse its suds off or get clean;
the eyes on the tallest box kites ask what it means
to feel you've come of age too late,
to crave, wherever you live, a change of scene.
Surf approaches but never touches the fire-eaters
on their buskers' ziggurat of sticks and stones.

Despite the alarming flapping sound,
a baby-blue, manta-ray-
shaped, lorry-sized parachute fabric contends
with itself; nearly spherical and improbably big,
a bubblegum-pink winged pig,
two feather-bearing dragons, a blue whale
and a square of colours inside colours glide
in parallel, so that they stay on the right side
of the spectator-safety exclusion zone.

The after-images the kite-strings leave
in the air over tidal flats seem not so much serene
as optimistic, even blithe,
as if they could believe
that civilisation was good for everyone.

The manta ray, now fully deflated, maintains
a series of cuts along its sleeve.
Somebody's boombox settles into the end
of the Velvet Underground's 'Who Loves the Sun',
then shifts to the Verlaines.

CAOIMHE MCKEOGH

Mr Bananafish

'What did you learn today, Mike?' Uncle Stanley asked as the boy tried to get his lunchbox into his bag.

'I'm Michael, not Mike,' said the little boy, who was almost the same size as his backpack. 'Mike means Mike B from Room Two and Mike N-J from Room Eight.'

'Oh.'

'I'm Mike-ill. I'm five so I'm in Room One.'

He finally got the bag zipped up around the bulge of lunchbox, stood and put it onto his back. He took Stanley's hand and Stanley smiled.

'What did you learn today, Mike-ill?'

They started walking out of the school.

'All the stars are suns,' Michael said, 'And the Big Bang made all the stars and then a tiny bit of the sun floated away and turned into Jupiter and then Jupiter made all the other planets.'

'Wow! Did they teach you that Pluto isn't a planet?'

Michael kicked a small stone and it skittered along the pavement ahead of them. 'Pluto isn't a planet.'

'When I went to school, they said Pluto was a planet. After I left, they changed their minds.'

'Where are we going?'

'To kindergarten, to get Nazel.'

'Hazel.'

'Who's Hazel?'

'My sister.'

'You have two! Are they twins?'

'Hazel's the only one.'

'I must have imagined Nazel. That's a shame. She was nice.'

'Ouch!' Michael started hopping, trying to grab the lifted foot with his spare hand. 'There's a stone in my sandal.'

'Well, don't dance about it! Sit down and take it out.'

'You can't sit on the pavement.'

'Yes you can. Look!'

Stanley sat down with his legs out in front of him. He took off his shoes, shook them upside down, then put them back on. The little boy sat down beside him and copied the routine.

'That's a big stone!' Stanley said. 'Why don't you wear shoes? I'm wearing shoes and I had no stones.'

'Grown-ups don't get stones in their shoes.'

'Oh, I didn't know that, but it makes perfect sense.'

The two stood and walked in silence for a while, holding hands, swinging their arms.

'How long until we get to Hazel's kindy?' asked Michael after a while.

'As long as it takes to walk a block.'

'Are you even a grown-up?' asked Michael.

'Yes,' Stanley said. 'Didn't you see how I had no stones in my shoes?'

'Then why can't you drive us in a car?'

'Because it's very sunny and sunshine helps children grow.'

'Is sunshine healthy?'

'Yes.'

'Mum says we have to wear sunscreen and a sunhat or we might get bits cut off our noses like Grandma if we're not careful.'

'Would they cut off the bit of your nose that you smell with?'

'That's your *whole* nose.'

'Well, that would make you look very strange, wouldn't it? That's the kindy across the road. Look both ways.'

As they crossed, Michael said, 'You're so old you thought Pluto was a planet.'

'I'm not old. I'm the same age as your mum.'

'Mum is seventy-three.'

'*Grandma* isn't even seventy-three.'

'Did they bring you back to school to tell you Pluto wasn't a planet?'

'No.' Stanley opened the gate to the kindergarten. 'Once you're gone, you're stuck with whatever they taught you.'

There weren't many children left at the kindergarten. Hazel ran to the door shouting, 'Uncle Banana! Uncle Ababababgagagadoodoo!'

She grabbed Stanley around his knees and he patted her head, saying, 'Careful, Hazel, you're a strong girl. If you knock me down, I might not get back up.'

'Abababgagagadoodoo,' said Hazel.

'That's her secret language,' Michael explained. 'It means she loves you.'

'What a shame that I can't speak it,' said Stanley. 'It sounds like a beautiful language. Now, Hazel, where's your bag?'

While the kindy teacher organised Hazel's belongings, Stanley carefully took his left arm out of the left sleeve of his yellow jumper, then his right arm out of the right sleeve, then he pulled the whole thing over his head. He tied it around his waist with two knots.

They set off walking again, all holding hands.

'How was kindy, Hazel?' asked Stanley.

She thought for a while. 'Spence fell off the climbing frame.'

'Was he okay?'

'No.'

'Oh dear!' said Stanley.

'It's all right,' said Hazel. 'I didn't like him very much.'

She let go of Stanley's hand for a second, turned around, and held on with her other hand, walking backwards.

'What animal year were you born in, Uncle Stanley?' asked Michael.

'Fish.'

'You can't be fish,' Michael said.

'What are you?'

'I'm dragon. Grandma is ox, Granddad is rat, Mummy is horse, and Hazel's horse, too.'

'Why can't I be a fish?'

'There's no fish.'

'I feel a lot like a fish,' Stanley sucked in his cheeks and made his mouth small and kissy.

Michael let go of Stanley's hand, stopped walking and stamped his foot. 'There's *no* fish.'

'I'm the only one. Do you have a stone in your sandal again?'

'Look!' said Hazel, pointing at the ground. 'Two nacorns.'

'Yes,' said Stanley, 'One is wearing a hat. Can you walk forwards from now on, please, Nazel?'

They paused for a second, while Hazel turned around, then kept walking.

'Where do nacorns get their hats?' asked Hazel.

'All acorns are born wearing hats,' said Stanley. 'Some of them lose their hats when they fall off the tree. But they never have to get their noses cut off.'

'Yeah, cause they hit the ground so hard their hats bounce away,' said Michael, running to catch up with them. 'And they don't *have* noses.'

'We're nearly home,' said Stanley.

'Not your home, *our* home,' said Michael, 'Mummy and Hazel and me.'

'Do you have a house?' asked Hazel.

'I'm going to share yours for the weekend.'

'Okay,' said Hazel. 'Do you like spiders?'

'Depends on their personality.'

'Mummy cries if she sees a spider,' said Michael, 'so I take them outside.'

'I cry if I see a spider too,' said Hazel. 'But I really like grapes.'

'This is us.' Stanley stopped walking and let go of the children's hands so he could take the key out of his pocket.

'Where did you get the key?' asked Michael.

'Your mum gave it to me.'

'Why?' asked Hazel.

'So we could get inside.'

'I miss Mummy,' said Hazel.

'No,' said Michael gently, kissing his sister on the cheek, 'You're okay.'

The phone rang. Mary glanced at the screen and then looked back to the road and let it ring. As soon as it stopped, it started again and she continued to ignore it. When it started for a third time, she accepted the call with a swipe of one finger, then connected it to the car's speakers with another swipe.

'Mum, I'm driving.'

A woman's voice came through the speakers: 'Mary, you make me so anxious. Why haven't you been answering my calls?'

She rolled her shoulders forwards and then backwards before she answered: 'I've been busy. I'm driving—I can't talk.'

'You're talking perfectly fine, Mary. Now, are you okay? I've been worried—'

'I have you on speakerphone and it's hard to hear you. Your voice is muffled.'

'I will speak very clearly, then,' her mother replied, very clearly.

'Oh, God, that's annoying! Just talk normally. But be quick—I'm using my phone for directions.'

'You're not using your phone for directions. Where are you going?'

'I'm having a weekend away.'

'Darling!'

'Don't shout at me, Mum. You're coming through the speakers, remember?'

'Mary! I'm so worried. Are you taking the children? Stanley seems to think—'

'I need some time to myself, Mum. I'm exhausted.'

'It's just, Mary, Stanley's saying he's—'

'Mum, don't get over-excited about it. I trust Stanley. They'll be fine.'

'Mary!'

'Don't shout at me, Mum!' Mary shouted. 'I decide who babysits my children. And if you keep shouting I'll hang up.'

'I would have flown down if you told me you needed a babysitter.'

'You said Stanley needed purpose in his life. He's been visiting every week. The kids love him.'

'Has he been doing the thing with lightbulbs and the windows?'

'Not at all. You can see him looking at them sometimes but he's trying so hard. The kids don't notice anything.'

'You've heard what he said to your father about the cat?'

'Yes, Mum, I heard.'

'Your father loves that cat, darling. He was so upset.'

'I can imagine.'

'Oh, he was a gorgeous boy, not so different from your Michael. I don't know what happened. I wish he'd been drafted into an army. You know, your father had a compulsory year in the military—'

'Yes, Mum, I know.'

'It shaped him, darling, it shaped him. If Stanley was a soldier, maybe he'd have a bit of perspective, a bit more self-discipline, and—'

'Mum, I don't want to talk about this right now.'

'Okay, darling, just—'

'What?'

'Don't let him drive with the children in the car.'

'Of course I won't.'

'Did you hide the keys?'

'I took the car. I told you, I'm driving right now.'

'I hope you realise he's not going to keep you updated. The kids could be in hospital and he still wouldn't phone. All his life he's never once phoned me or sent a message. It's always me who has to call him, and I have to do it twenty times before he'll pick up.'

'It annoys him when you do that. That's why he says such awful things on the phone. Like about Dad's cat ...'

'Oh, he wasn't just *saying* that. He meant it. Your father could tell by the tone of his voice.'

'Mum, I need to go.'

'You promise he's not behaving strangely?'

'He's been lovely, Mum.'

'Even with the li—'

'Even with the lightbulbs,' Mary interrupted. 'There's only one little thing I noticed. He's got this yellow jumper he won't take off.'

'But it's summer.'

'I know. He says he doesn't want the children to see the scars from when he broke his arm and the bone ripped through the skin.'

'He's never broken his arm.'

'I know.' Mary giggled. 'It's sweet, though. The kids call him Uncle Banana.'

'That's not funny, it's horrible. I'm going to fly down tomorrow.'

The giggling stopped immediately. 'Mum. If you turn up at my house uninvited and you undermine my choice of babysitter, I'll never talk to you again.'

'Mary—'

'He needs to know that we trust him, Mum. I'll be back on Sunday.'

'You'll phone me when you get home?'

'I'll try.'

'No, promise me.'

'I'll *try* to remember to call you on Sunday. Give my love to Dad.'

'Mary!'

She hung up with another swipe of her finger, then turned off the phone and drove on in silence.

The children followed an unspoken routine: sandals off, backpacks on hooks, lunchboxes by the kitchen sink. They used the toilet one after the other, then washed their hands semi-simultaneously, and ended up sitting at the dining table staring at Stanley. Stanley stood in the doorway and stared back.

'What's for afternoon snacks?' asked Michael when he sensed that nothing was forthcoming.

'Your mum said fruit,' Stanley offered. 'And bread if you were extra hungry.'

'With honey or jam or both?' asked Hazel.

'She said no honey or jam, only butter and Marmite.'

The children groaned.

'Just fruit then,' said Michael in a tortured voice.

Stanley went to the kitchen and took out a wooden chopping board and a big silver knife. He cut an orange into four wedges and an apple into eight slices, and peeled a banana before cutting it into a handful of coins. He divided it all equally between two plastic bowls and carried them out to the table.

'Water in a purple cup,' said Hazel.

'And a green cup,' said Michael.

Stanley went back to the kitchen. The purple cup was in the dishwasher, covered with yoghurt, so he ran it under the tap for a while, rubbing it with his fingers until the yoghurt was gone. He filled both cups with water and went back to the table.

The children had orange quarters pushed in behind their lips, stretching their mouths into uncomfortable-looking shapes.

'Look!' Michael tried to say, and it came out like 'Gooh.' He pulled the orange out of his mouth and tried again, 'Look, Uncle Stanley, look at Hazel! Did you see me?'

'I saw you both. You're bananas,' Stanley laughed.

Hazel pulled out her orange slice. 'We're not bananas, we're people,' she said. 'We're Hazel and Michael.'

'"Bananas" is a friendly way of saying someone's crazy,' Stanley said.

'Then you're the only banana,' the girl told him very seriously. 'Uncle Banana.'

'You're Mr Banana,' Michael suggested. 'Everyone calls you banana.'

'You're Mr BananaFISH,' Hazel added.

'It's amazing you say that, because I was telling your brother earlier how I'd like to be a fish.'

'Mr Bananafish! Mr Bananafish!' the two children chanted, and then laughed with their heads thrown back and their whole bodies involved.

'You can't be the boss of us if you're a banana,' Hazel giggled. 'You're not a grown-up.'

'Yeah,' Michael agreed in a disappointed voice, 'You're not even seventy-three. Do you have a work?'

Stanley unknotted his jumper from his waist, pulled it back over his head and pushed his arms through the sleeves.

'Maybe we could have honey on bread after all,' he said, 'if everyone sits quietly and eats their fruit without being silly.'

'Abagabeee Mr Bananafish,' said Hazel.

'That was silly, Hazel,' said Stanley.

'Why are you being mean now?' asked Michael.

'I'm being sensible,' said Stanley.

'I miss Mummy,' said Hazel, resting her chin on the table next to her bowl of fruit.

'Mummy said we can't have honey,' said Michael. 'Why are you breaking the rules?'

'For a special treat,' said Stanley. 'It's okay to have honey as a treat.'

'Aboojah,' said Hazel sadly.

'If you keep talking like that, Hazel, you won't get the rest of your fruit, let alone any honey on bread.'

'Then she'll be hungry,' said Michael. 'She's trying to grow.'

'Who's the boss around here, Michael?' asked Stanley, 'It's me! I'm a grown-up, and you're only five years old.'

Hazel stood up on her chair so she was almost the height of Stanley's chin, and she shouted, 'Mummy is the boss around here, Mr Bananafish, and if you are mean and you give us nothing to eat we will tell her.' She sat down again, looking quite pleased, then added quietly, 'You won't be coming back.'

Stanley leaned down and kissed her tiny nose. 'I'm sorry, I won't be mean to you any more.'

'What about me?' asked Michael.

Stanley kissed his finger and reached across the table to touch it onto Michael's nose. 'I will be very nice to you too, Michael.'

'Abagagadeedee,' said Hazel.

'She loves you again,' said Michael.

Stanley kissed Hazel once on the forehead and then once on each cheek, and she giggled and scrunched up her face. He tried to kiss her mouth and she pulled her head away and said, 'Hey!'

'Hey, yourself. Are you finished with your fruit?'

'No.'

'Then you'd better be quick or I'll start eating it. You too, Michael.'

The children started eating their fruit again, orange juice and banana slime covering their fingers and chins, and Stanley watched them for a while.

'I'm going to get myself a snack,' he said, and walked to the kitchen.

He tried to put an apple into the pocket of his shorts but it wouldn't fit, so he put a banana in instead. He went out the front door, locked it behind him, and walked up the path to the street. A woman was walking past with a small black dog. She looked up and smiled.

'There's no need to laugh at my nose,' he told her.

'Excuse me?' the woman said.

'I have a normal nose. Don't stare. If you want to see a strange nose, take a look at my mother, or at your dog. There's nothing wrong with my nose.'

The woman crossed the road and walked away quickly.

Stanley put the key to Mary's house into her mailbox, then took his cellphone out of his back pocket and put that in too. He pulled the sleeves of his yellow sweater down over his hands and ran in a stiff, upright way to the bus stop on the corner where a bus had just pulled up.

'Will you get me to the ferry terminal by 4.30?' he asked the driver.

'I go to the station,' the driver said. 'It's a half-hour walk to the ferry from there.'

'I'd prefer to go to the ferry terminal,' Stanley said 'Do the trains go far?'

'This isn't a taxi,' the driver said, then added, 'Trains will take you anywhere in the North Island, eventually.'

'That'll have to do,' said Stanley. 'One ticket to the end of the line, please.'

He sat in the front row and peeled the banana he'd been keeping in his pocket, then ate it in three big bites, barely chewing, so it pushed down his throat in slimy lumps.

He looked down at the empty skin in his hand as suburbs bumped past outside his window, then he yelled to the driver, 'Stop the bus!'

'Next stop is half a minute away,' the driver said, without looking back.

'I'll be sick on the floor,' said Mr Bananafish, waving the peel.

The bus lurched to a halt and the double doors jerked open, hissing.

Stanley leapt off. He dropped the banana skin, already browning, in the gutter full of leaves.

He peeled himself—the big jumper over his head in seconds—then tied the sleeves in a knot around his neck.

He ran back the way the bus had come, as fast as he could, hoping no spiders had visited while he was gone. His yellow jumper billowed behind him, rippling with speed.

ADITYA VASUDEVAN

Smoking Koans

The flush bones on the sides of my feet press into the carpet, my backside into the cushion asymmetrically, slight tension in the hips and knees, which are rigid from a night's sleep. I can hear the soft susurrus of cars on the main road, the aggressive plod of a bus then the wobbling clank of a lorry whose load is too loosely fixed to its infrastructure. Then quiet. The automated bug spray ejaculates its plume. Then the cars start again.

Focus on the breath

Try to focus on the breath. If distractions arise, note them; they'll fade.

I see the backs of my eyelids swimming. I try to gently focus on my nostrils where the air is passing in and out, as if pushing my consciousness forwards from the inside of my skull. I detect the coolness of air coming in and the warmth of air going out: the *out* is somehow muted and incorporeal compared to the *in*. This telescopic attention immediately makes my breathing manual, contrived. I try to step back from forced, intentional breathing—searching for instinct or automation. My outbreath recedes further. Where's it gone?

Television's favourite crooked lawyer leans cartoonishly forward and to the left with plaintive hands, soundlessly explaining. The triangle of negative space above his back and shoulders folds like origami paper, erasing him. Chest rising, manual breathing, balloon full again: let it go.

Remember to note distractions. But not like some spiritual game of whack-a-mole. Identify them. Understand them. Let them go.

Viscous and deliberate inbreath, empty outbreath. 'Have you been telling porkies?'—slightly chubby face, derisive smile looking down at me. 'What?' 'Pork pies—you were meant to be in afterschool care.' 'I ... I don't know ...' Shame, shame like they threw rocks at you in the street, a deadweight in the solarplexus. 'But I've never been to afterschool care,' I should've said. 'I'm afraid of what will happen to me there'—hiding instead in the gym with its lines for basketball and lines for netball and lines for indoor football, twisting around me like shopping mall directions but with no 'You are Here'. Note it. Watching the memory, his chubby, derisive face is below me—he's short!—and his (chubby, derisive) face is almost kind, seeking understanding through banter, banter I didn't understand then. Note: mental talk.

Children with blue blazers and rows of badges exiting library doors, faces stolen above the mouths of collars; badly knotted ties that get loosened every day at 3.15pm and tightened every morning at 8.30am, never re-tied, popped over heads like colourful nooses. Afterschool care is where you go when you're not picked up on time. If you know you're going, it's a routine. If you don't know you're going, it's like abandonment. I breathe it out. A loud lorry kachugging down the main road. Mental image. Mental talk.

You could've just gone and sat in the library like everyone else and not felt the sting of abandonment or shame—signed the form, found a corner, read a book. *Stop ...*

I threw a rugby ball at Rory's head once. I can't remember if I ran away immediately or if he kicked me hard in the shins first. Maybe that was years later, in high school, no blue blazers but maroon sweaters instead. It feels like a victory, the spinning rugby ball leaving my right hand (on a loop, repeated, slow motion), hurtling with unapologetic rage at his smug face. He ducks just in time. He looks to his accomplice as if this provides justification to torture me for another week. I don't care. I've let something out rather than pressing down down down with the base of my palm, kneading the dough. It's my first act of outward existence, of not apologising. I'm here. My being here is brute fact; deal with it.

A slight twinge of pain in my right knee at the bend. Consider its intensity, how long you've felt it. Know it will pass.

I return to the breath, broader focus this time. My chest and shoulders rise with the balloon. I cross the mountain's peak for everything to come down softer, gentler. Then up again, this time less effort and less intention, then down again, this time calmer, already soft. I hear a car that sounds like a spaceship powering up, as if surrounded by rock-concert smoke. Then, I catch the rollerskating papier-mâché image as it comes in. Catching its inception is exhilarating, like balancing on a sound wave or boating off the mythological edge of the world. I follow the skater as several torn pieces of paper, his image jumping from one to another.

Interruption: my wife's footsteps from the bedroom to the bathroom. I hear the door close, the bathroom fan come on.

Cars again. Motorbike grunts first. The sound of distance: between road, trees, back yard, house, space and self. Picture beams of celestial light cut by tree branches then window grates projected onto a parallelogram of floor. The tide of breath goes out and in, '*the wheels on the bus go …*'

I'm sitting on the patterned seat of a bus—the same design all over the country, usually featuring coloured confetti—looking out the window as the bus mounts roundabouts and attempts to murder pedestrians. I'm sealed in with black headphones, framed by the window and the seats in front of me. My knees point towards the window politely so that others are not intimidated out of sitting next to me. My knees point towards the window because they do not otherwise fit into the space provided.

My organs bump against my ribs every time the bus jolts. The whole bus shakes with the driver's dissatisfaction with her job. I sniffle into my hands; wipe my hands on my pants. My hayfever worsens and I start having to wipe my hands on the straps of my backpack, but discreetly, so strangers cannot pass judgement on my hygiene.

I see a kinaesthetic image of my nose as it takes in and lets out air, on the dioramic scale that would be used to teach medical students about the olfactory system. The tree branches on my road open like legs for the powerlines. It's quite a sight. See the bus. See the trees. They are concrete, clear. Exhale.

The bathroom door creaks open again and she goes back to the bedroom. The creak echoes: bedroom door. I imagine I hear her walk to the bed and slump back into its comfort, frog-shaped under the blanket as usual. Her comfort warms me. An image of her face blissfully smushed into the pillow, retreating back to rest from the harsh white bathroom light.

The knee joint is still a little tight. The corner bones of my feet a little numb.

'*I get byyy, with a little help from my friends, I get hiiigh with a little help from my …*'

I sit on the sun-baked balcony with a beer looking out over the trees and the motorway telling Mikaela 'how good' it all is as Stephen plays a song from inside the flat and the curtains gently flap in the wind. Everyone has finished exams. They're all wearing bright shorts. I have a tendency to do that (say 'how good') and narrate the present moment, or describe it back to those living it, as if the naming and containing of the experience somehow enriches it, secures its place in the right side of memory.

Or maybe I do it to add to the tally of what is good.

Reel it in.

I close my eyes tighter and slow my brain down. I take a deep breath in on count one and let it out in a big ball on count two. I fill the balloon on count three until it can't take any more, and push it out through my nose on count four.

'Oṃ bhūr bhuvaḥ svaḥ. Tát savitúr váreṇyaṃ. Bhárgo devásya dhīmahi. Dhíyo yó naḥ pracodáyāt.' I whisper these words to myself before my interview with the best law firm in the country. I don't believe the mantra, or understand it, but it's inscribed in my memory from my early teens. I'm meant to say it every day. Despite my best efforts, the words only find my mouth when my nerves are stretched to the length of a mythical bow and tugged to the tune of amplified feedback and static. My best efforts are to never say it. Nonetheless I am calmed by it; I get the job. I talk about the marketplace, my interest in satirical news, pretend to know how law firms work, ask questions. Display confidence and a willingness to exist without apologising.

I feel the image dimming, washed over with watercolours and the feeling of red brick and cut grass rising. It's not the shifting ink on a Rorschach test. It's not the overlapping waves on a graph. It's not a star-wipe or a cross-fade, or even the camera turning a corner. I cross the threshold into school grounds, everything in miniature. The fields that once provoked stitches and panting are barely 500m wide. The two-storey block of classrooms, once a skyscraper, looks quaint. The bell rings. Halflings in blazers and badges and severely knotted ties stream out into the open space beaming joy out of every pore: it is the end of the day. My old teachers emerge and I shrink and wrinkle like oversoaked skin, hiding behind my mother who's half my size and hardly a barricade. The oxygen here is oppressive. 'Have you been telling pork-pies again?' I don't know why I was scared of afterschool care when I was here, but my face blanched and every volitional part of me gooped with the viscous treacle of anxiety; I don't know why I hid in the gym either. We spot the target—my little brother with his bob of straight hair, equal to the joy around him—charging down stairs and tugging on friends' backpacks, his long school socks characteristically pooled at his ankles.

Flipped view, not mine: through the car window you can see my brother crack open a bag of Grainwaves, sour cream and chives. We tussle in the back seat and I steal a few. The car is blurred. I have drifted. I try not to reprimand myself for drifting: not whack-a-mole. Count one inhale deeply no room left in the balloon (lack of oxygen) count two come down relax shoulders exhale tension. Am I doing this right? I've forgotten how to breathe normally.

The other knee now tightens in conversation with the first. Acutely aware of tendons in thighs and groin. Bum numb.

Find the bottom of the exhale count three and realise it is continuous with the previous breath, fill the rosy pink balloons count four release. Mental focus narrows to the tunnels of my nostrils as the wind blows through them, back and forth. The cold air riles the nostril walls more than the warm. An internal blueprint is echolocated from nostril throat diaphragm to stomach, cradle to grave, and back again, flown through by infinitessimally small crows slaloming in unison, an unbroken chain of distinct parts operating as one, a school of fish balled together, vibrating, protecting itself from predators by each electrically charged fish knowing the mind of its neighbour and its neighbour and its neighbour and so on—the school the flock the body, only a container. For a moment, all physical experience is breath.

A tightness in my chest enters the landscape. It's Sunday morning. Work starts again tomorrow. You're as far as you can conceptually be from next weekend. You've squandered the only precious time you had to read, to write, to feel unburdened. But put that kind of pressure on free time and it becomes the greatest weight: every option is chained to the indeterminacy of opportunity cost. Perhaps all you're capable of is wanting freedom when you're unable to have it. Perhaps it's better to leave it alone: an oasis of untapped potential, a perfect circle, unactualisable. *Stop*, mental talk. Monday looms, but it's only 11am. I try to separate it: the feeling in my chest is physical; the prospect of tomorrow's meaninglessness is prospect only. Exhale.

The shins of my chicken-legs are bruised from lunchtime. The other boys are passing a hacky sack back and forth in the B-block corridor. Rory sends one like a missile at my face, which narrowly misses. Some willing associate retrieves the errant sack and passes it back to Rory, who takes a second pass—this time nailing me in the stomach. Show no pain, teeth gritted. I quickly pick up the hacky sack before another lackey reaches it. Ice cold, I pop it out the closest second-floor window—'oy, what the hell?!' they screech in unison. A pause where my fear threatens to triumph—'sorry, I'm a dick'. A glorious boyish chorus of 'ooooooooh' echoes down the corridor: the colosseum quickly shifting its loyalty. Rory tries visibly not to look beaten. The memory fades naturally, a deep breath out.

A blank screen. Looking at the backs of your eyelids is different to looking inwards. Memory is up, physical is forward. Imagination is also up.

A gargoyle rendered as in an 8-bit video game flies above Queenstown, above Wanaka, weaving through hilltops. I am stationed behind it as it flies, following its lead. I breathe deeply, see the backs of my eyelids, then the bird again, now rendered gloriously, like an eagle from *Lord of the Rings*. It opens its wings to an orchestral swell. The comforting shine of sun off blue water below, guided on either side by rows of snow-capped peaks. This landscape is a persona, a welcome.

Do nothing

I wonder how long it's been. I must be at least halfway through. Time to shift gears: 'Do nothing'. Don't worry about the breath, just let whatever happens happen. If you notice an intention to control your attention, drop it.

My mind immediately clears. Absolute focus on the breath becomes second nature. I hear the cars again, sound rising and falling as they pass the house.

The mind's a petulant child. Ask it to focus on the breath and it'll shake your hand, say 'Of course, would be my pleasure', and proceed down every lacuna of memory and imagination available. Ask it to do whatever it pleases, and it'll say 'Of course, how kind of you', and become empty, stretching barren in all directions like the Sahara.

I breathe calmly, easily, my attention on the tunnels of my nose. I feel now the minute vibrations of my nostril hairs as air comes in, and the wind tunnel reversed, upside down, as the air goes out. An olfactory diorama.

Rolling green hills bisected by wooden fences and dotted with cows. The road is adjacent to an old train line. The road is adjacent to a river also. We pass the Māori cemetery that goes up the mountainside, where the newly dead return to their ancestors in the soil. I would be more at home if you cremated me and scattered my ashes in the adjacent river than if you flew me back to my ancestors. I feel like an old Japanese river spirit for a river that's been filled in. Good thing I'm an atheist. Good thing it ends for me definitively. Otherwise I'd be searching good and hard for a Koan of salvation.

Little islands of light become visible on the backs of my eyelids, a dim ultrasound. I follow them as they warp and disappear. I'm meant to appreciate their passing, both their flow and disappearance. Detect the intention: a punctuation mark in mid-air. Drop it.

The opening notes of my timer's alarm, designed and selected to be gentle, an incremental return to the day, are jarring. The sound is close by (my phone in front of me), but that's not the problem: the same alarm wakes me up every morning. My brain and body know from the first three notes alone—the jingle's leitmotif—that it's time. There is no jolt of awakening anxiety. I greet my return.

I open my eyes. The light is warm and lush through the trees. The coffee table resolves itself, along with the bookshelves, the plants and the blank television. I unfold my legs, careful with their stiffness. I make a coffee and the day unfurls.

TOM WESTON

Politics

We are, all of us, compromised.
We are alive and we are compromised.

We have put our scruples aside.
Exile is our brand.

In order to survive on earth, we have
put our scruples aside.

We are alive; we are survivors.
The people's democratic benevolence

is a rusty fake.
The wise ruler, the harmonious way,

the balm of prosperity, its drug,
they are all fake.

We are alive; we are certain.
We are, all of us, compromised.

Call out for help, wave your arms.
Do you think the lifeguard really cares?

Does the leader care?
The leader is busy growing huge.

Take my arm; pull me aboard.
I am coming with you.

REBECCA BALL

Ikatere

at the bottom of the hill
Ikatere, grandson of Tangaroa,
plays on a beach made of stones

he sinks his hands into them
warm from the sun
fallen shards of mountains
rolled round and smooth
by the tongue of the ocean

quick as a fish he scoops
dry stones into dry hills
digs down down down
until his fingers find water

he shows me the stones
beneath the surface
cool and dark
glistening like roe

BEN EGERTON

Calibration

Who can ascend
these hills, o Lord?

And how quickly? Who
has a stubborn heart

and sure feet
and a strong GPS signal?

I look at Dai: *Ready?*
That sounds like something

I might have written,
he replies. I should've known

he doesn't use
a fancy watch. And he's got

those sandals
like the Tarahumara wear,

those barefoot running ones
all the rage a while back.

After all his run-less years
Dai's calves

still hold their definition
but his middle

has spread a bit—
a middle that never once

bore the weight
of another

king's armour; calves
to deliver him

from lion, bear, giant;
the balls
to invite
another man's wife

to his bed—so we have
one thing in common

at least. *Don't you miss*
being outside? I ask.

That's why I write about
it all the time, he says.

CLAIRE ORCHARD

Unravelling things

That Ernest Rutherford is a past member of the Manchester Literary
and Philosophical Society I learn from studying the plaque
in the hallway of their new headquarters. I'm just in time
for a public lecture on John Dalton's atomic theory of 1803
as it relates to our current understanding of atomic physics.
Today's speaker is a man I've never heard of, but as he has

the voice of my grandfather I'm inclined to listen when he says
all matter—you, me, in fact everything in this room (I'm looking
now at the dyed brown hair on the back of the head of the woman
in front of me)—is composed of atoms. Well, almost everything,
he tacks on apologetically. The sound of my voice, your thoughts
and feelings about what you're experiencing—he shakes his own

balding head—these are not things, at least not in the atomic sense.
He moves swiftly on—there will be time for questions at the end—
to the 'Big Bang', that mysterious event, thirteen-point seven billion
years ago, when pure energy was converted into elementary particles.
He pauses, shuffles his notes; here come the meat and potatoes.
The first part of John Dalton's atomic theory states that atoms

are indivisible and indestructible. Of course—he says this bit
with a downward twist of his lips—we have accepted
for a while now this is not the case, that a nuclear reaction
can create or destroy matter, given of course we define matter as solely
its mass and not the energy such a reaction releases. As far as we know,
energy cannot be created or destroyed; it can only be transformed

from one state—hand gesture, a sweep left to right—to another.
We also know that, when we die, we become the quintessential
recyclable: our atoms, released—opening hand movement—
merely relocate to new real estate, allowing us to become perhaps
part leaf, part stereo dial, part some soft small animal, this time
one with a tail. In this sense we are only ever on loan to ourselves,

all of us having, at some time, been part star and who knows
some day—wry smile—we may be again. He stops to check
his watch. Time now for questions and I sense there are many.
That, as usual, there will not be time enough to answer them all.
The man next to me wonders aloud if time passing is another non-thing,
in an atomic sense. If only getting to know these things felt like enough.

MARY CRESSWELL

Route 66

The time capsule slows
pulls over to the shaky shack
with gas pumps in front

We scramble in and out
through the desert sun
into the shack, gathering

at the zinc oasis, a red tank
full to eye level with dusty water
bottles of tepid drinks

Out back gila monsters
wait, frozen in their cages
indifferent to the sun

next to the rattlesnake
who is almost about to blink
but it's time to get back in the car.

ANGELA TROLOVE

Braided Rivers—Water Tumbles and Slips

Fennel, yarrow, plantain, gorse and blue borage grow out of cat-litter shingle beneath the Torlesse Range. Grass, driftwood, thistles, poppies, pinecone cores, dandyweed, lambs-ear and broom all people this backwater—the Eyre River.

By the river's edge, a ring of stones apports black cinders. Water runs east, limpid and scarce under the run of stones, the water giddy and gentle and single-minded. Grey stones are white-marbled. Silt tucks under both vegetable and mineral. Yellow fennel seeds brush at knee height, fresh and short, or high and scab brown. A swallow licks along the river and a fantail ferries itself across to unfocused willows. Poplars too are bare, but they're tagged with reluctant leaves against the blue-grey fog-horn sky.

By the water, a fennel tap-root lies exposed, the long green parsnip of it, parchment dry. Skeletal leaves and raffia are nabbed in a silt sod, hauled up easily by the shoulder barge of rushing water on high rain.

This river repositions itself every year. It lies here in its run of shingle, it lies there. It's more or less in the middle. Secure plants—plants that need only a moment's notice to sprout—these are the plants of which this river's botanic profile is composed. The river runnels newly every winter, and in the dry season wildflowers camp up the dry floor. Braided rivers are the native rivers of the South Island. Braided rivers are shallow, inconstant, wild and strangely fertile: the recourse of rural adolescents.

Two black and white ducks scud their cries as they fly. They arrive at the bank to forage.

Fresh yarrow smells like honey and attics, dried yarrow smells the same. Pink yarrow smells like camphor. Poppies are yet squinting closed, nestled in their carrot-tops. Dock and daisies languish. Rocks smudge, clatter and scramble like dice underfoot. An uprooted willow has netted straws, fibres, twigs, a plank and fragile gorse—all grey—and even a burnt log.

Fleas jump. Swallows spar. Ducks whinge. The stream mumbles through an incomplete stone dam, plopping and swishing, middle-aged, funnelling and twisting, always buckling with the same surprise as the water that flowed earlier.

The ducks face each other and sag their voices in unison. After a while they turn apart, one shakes and the other looks at the stones, stepping away.

The water tumbles and slips, its perfect tension unbroken, and each rock wears its darker tideline of their history, the water-meets-rock history, still living that encounter.

JAMES MCNAUGHTON

Night Swim

Heaved low into the sky
three nights past her prime

a chunk missing, dirty yellow,
sick of being

shone on.
Over the hill

I walked to the black face
of rock above the bay

shielded from the bleach
of lamplight. Unsurveilled

in that magic place
of reprieve

in shadow deep
as silence after noise

stars appeared
to warm the foaming breakers.

The moon had gone, left her
wrinkled silver garment floating.

RUTH CORKILL

The Garden Party

Sometimes I catch that girl
who sat with eyes glazed over
so far gone out the back door
into estuaries and gullies
that she doesn't hear the call for dinner.

I thought of her this afternoon.
Around the table were all blusterers,
highly coloured like nothing on this earth.
The thought was a fleeting thing
but absolute like a bird recognised
the same instant it disappeared.
A starling! I saw a starling
under the ngaio—

After the guests had gone
I found someone's handkerchief
inside my bedside book. Presumably yours.

I didn't think much of your friend.
You look so bewildered and elsewhere except
when your smile for him breaks open,
like a poppy fidgeting out of its casing
on a hot afternoon. You know,

I used to hear music and conversation
in empty rooms as you do.
I did not call them angels.

RIA MASAE

Papālagi

I.

Walking through a village in Samoa
the excited tamaiti crowded around,
their grinning eyes and perfect teeth
chanting, *Pālagi, Pālagi, Pālagi!*

Pālagi
[1] white person / European

I faltered, confused
then replied, *Leai, leai, o a`u o Samoa.*
But they laughed
as if I had revealed a childish fantasy.

Pālagi
[2] foreigner

II.

Perhaps it was the European ship's cannons
exploding the serenity of the tropical air and Pacific waves
that caused the Samoan people to turn towards the sea
when they first laid their brown eyes
on a gigantic bird with white wings
gliding across the ocean towards them.
When the great white bird waded ashore
and from it pale-skinned creatures alighted onto the sand,
my people thought the sky had exploded
and the ghostly beings had descended from the Heavens.

The word Pālagi derives from Papālagi.

*Pā/papā
  explode/explodes (plural), explosions
*Lagi
  sky

[3] Papālagi
exploding sky

If only my people had known
gods do not announce their arrival
with the noise of gunpowder and iron.

When the missionaries came ... they had the Bible and we had the land.
They said 'Let us pray.' We closed our eyes. When we opened them,
we had the Bible and they had the land.—Desmond Tutu

WEN-JUENN LEE

returning home again

I imagine returning in pillared light
cute, like Reese Witherspoon
in *Sweet Home Alabama*
upstaging backwater houses
made of pure salt, everyone
in wide-eyed close-ups:
you've changed.
        But my road to Damascus begins
        not with estranged husbands
        but the Johnsonville Line & us shrieking
        CLITORIS!
                after Year 12 biology
                baiting rheumy-eyed businessmen
                to sigh
                        Thank God
                when we leave
                our shoes & dirty sex.
                        Here, we were feral & blind, we were
                        hurtling from some devil school—
                        and if a train curves blindly from
                        Point A to B, home was
                        seven stops shifting in smelly-feet
                        carriages, the art of slipping lolly bags
                        between mossy transport seats
forget the girls
who will be new & intimidating
the train conductor who will call me
'ma'am'
        somewhere between tunnelled light

and Ngaio Gorge blushing green
the wind will say
remember
    how your body & mine
    cradled distance with open hands?
remember
    how you told me
    you would never get sick of this place?

ANTON BLANK

Racism and Hope

It is noticeable for me that life is changing—slowly for the more conservative and rapidly for the far-sighted. The root of the change lies in the transference from a system of mutual reciprocity to that of a money economy.—Arapera Blank, 1958[1]

When my mother wrote these words, Māori had been migrating from their rural homelands to the city in search of work for almost two decades. In response to this shift, government policy sought to turn Māori into British citizens. The dream was that Māori and Pākehā would be united as New Zealanders; no brown or white, just honey-coloured Kiwis all. A policy of pepper-potting Māori Affairs houses into white suburbs actively discouraged the residential concentration of Māori, and in 1960 the Hunn Report famously recommended that New Zealand move beyond assimilation to integration.[2] Māori have challenged these policies and resisted the politics of power inherent in this rhetoric, however, and over time this Māori resistance has come to sit centrally in our national identity.

Later in the 1960s Brazilian philosopher Paolo Freire published his seminal text *Pedagogy of the Oppressed*, and formally ushered in a postcolonial paradigm. Freire explored the power dynamics of oppression, and how oppressed groups are absorbed and lulled into colonial systems. Rather than being a state of emancipation, freedom, according to Freire, is in and of itself a continual process; it is 'the quest for human completion'.[3] Racism, therefore, is a macro-political issue that is exercised through power dynamics and Freire's influence cannot, in my view, be underestimated. It has been very influential in the development of Māori discourse; and in this schema education is not and cannot be a neutral phenomenon because it articulates and maintains the prevailing hegemony.

Logically, then, if we wanted to create better outcomes for Māori, we needed to shift the power dynamic to include Māori decisionmaking, and change the discourse to reflect Māori values and understandings. Across the spectrum of public enterprise and service, this has been the approach adopted by Māori influencers and workforces for more than fifty years. The development of kaupapa Māori education, the establishment of the Waitangi Tribunal, more Māori in Parliament, the incorporation of Māori models into health and justice strategies—these evolutions symbolise the postcolonial period and Māori rejection of the assimilation narrative.

This *modus operandi* hit the public service shortly after I started a career in social work with the Department of Social Welfare in 1985. Two consecutive reports, the most well known being John Rangihau's *Puao-Te-Ata-Tu*,[4] argued that the department was rife with institutional racism. Its policies and practices discriminated against Māori and as a result Māori were over-represented as beneficiaries of the state's income support and social work interventions. Anti-racism aficionados had bandied the term 'institutional racism' about in previous decades and, following on from Rangihau's report, it would become part of the vernacular. Fifty years on, there has in fact been a veritable resurgence of the paradigm, which is now discussed as a matter of course on the fourth estate. Despite these developments, if our revolutionary goal way back when was the emancipation of Māori—so that Māori experienced more freedom and less subjugation—the vision is at best only partially realised.

There is certainly more visible indigenous leadership and participation in the bourgeois industries that determine the type of life Māori can expect to have. Across justice, health, education and social services, the Māori workforce is not insignificant and in pockets is actually quite sizeable. A third of the staff of Oranga Tamariki (the government's Ministry for Children), for example, is Māori. We have emerged out of the postcolonial protest period, when we were very much outside the tent of decisionmaking, to be part of the apparatus we set out to attack and deconstruct. The discussion inside these institutions has also changed to incorporate anti-racist and Māori ways of being, communication and autonomy. The Treaty of Waitangi provides the basis for the approach to Māori issues for government ministries and agencies. Use of and interest in te reo Māori are flourishing.

Given these evolutions, can Māori live the life they value and can they share in the capitalist bounty? A cursory glance at the data suggests that any abundance of capitalism is still far from evenly shared. Most Māori live in the poorest areas and suburbs,[5] we trail behind Pākehā in education, and are one of the most imprisoned populations in the world.[6] Our rates of suicide are the highest in the country.[7] I could go on to describe trends in other areas, but it would make for a long and depressing litany of social malaise. Suffice to say that the Māori profile mirrors that of African Americans—and indigenous populations all over the world. Having expended so much energy, as the Māori and government sectors have, on addressing institutional racism, the question of why there hasn't been more significant change remains. We continue to apply the same strategies to transform the system even when the evidence suggests that up until now, most of the time the strategies have achieved diddly-squat.

Postcolonialism signalled a shift in perspective and approach, situating the locus of racism in the political and social worlds, away from being seen as an interpersonal issue. Rectifying the outcomes of racism necessitated a de- and re-construction of systems, approaches, values and narratives. This lofty mission is actually quite esoteric, so while the system change is visible and audible, there hasn't been enough attention paid to the workforces responsible for implementing the strategies. We have expected workers to support new approaches without first explaining why their existing behaviours are faulty and detrimental. And second, we haven't explained what a new way of being is. Teachers spend less time with Māori students. Police staff are more likely to arrest Māori than other groups. Doctors spend less time with Māori patients.[8] I have worked across these sectors and when these patterns are pointed out, for the most part, workers are shocked by and cannot explain their own behaviour. Altruistically motivated workers don't realise or want to believe that they are depriving Māori of their rights, entitlements and freedom.

Implicit bias has also been introduced into public discussion as a way of explaining the patterns I have described. The science of bias is unpopular with pockets of Māori, who argue that racism is a conscious behaviour. I also believe that racism is a conscious belief and practice (that one race is superior to another or others). I don't believe, however, that New Zealand teachers are marching into schools every day to intentionally exclude Māori students. More likely, the evidence suggests that teachers are on automatic pilot and influenced by biases and attitudes sitting just below the level of their conscious awareness.[9] The behaviour is, therefore, implicit rather than deliberate.

When the implicit bias is exposed, when workers see it in themselves and the system that surrounds them, then change is possible. The situation becomes more complex and urgent as our population diversifies and new groups bring their understanding and interpretation of Māori behaviours and abilities to the table. Part of our postcolonial dream was tino rangatiratanga, self-determination and the establishment of Māori systems, but the reality is that most of the time, most Māori students won't be taught by Māori teachers. The principal of a low-decile Auckland school told me last year that even new migrant teachers are telling her that Māori children can't learn.

Applying these models to myself, I really begin to understand the psychology of racism and bias. This has become a very important aspect of my own development, a Freirian 'quest for human completion', if you will. Have I ever had a racist thought? Yes, I have. Have I ever used racist language? Yes, I have, but not intentionally, and in some situations I was unaware of specific sensitivities about race and language. Am I aware of stereotypes about other ethnicities and groups and have I ever responded to someone on the basis of a stereotype? Most definitely I have. Does ignorance excuse my behaviour? No, but once my ignorance has been exposed, I can behave differently.

Over the past five years I have become increasingly interested in racism as an interpersonal and psychological issue. When I acknowledge it in myself, I am more able to be compassionate towards the workforces that engage inadequately with whānau Māori. It is the dimension that we have missed as we have focused our attention on systems and power structures. It is also the point where change is now most urgently required.

I am not convinced that confrontational approaches to racism are productive. Having survived anti-racism education across a number of professions, my experience is that the approach creates a chasm. Māori feel aggrieved and belligerent; it's a very othering and divisive process. Pākehā are intimidated, and even when they are sympathetic the confrontation paralyses them into inactivity. As Māori, we abandon these workforces, and leave them to their own devices at our own peril. There needs to be a way forward (dare I repeat an overused cliché?), a partnership approach to racism that is both conciliatory and proactive. I feel a sense of urgency about the situation, especially as it pertains to education, as the population of Māori and Pasifika children continues to swell in our schools.

When we explore and address racism and bias as an aspect of the human condition and psychology that we can change and modify, we open up a way forward. As Māori it is important that we continue to lead these discussions, because we have experienced racism in all its permutations over many decades and understand its impact, whether it is intentional, implicit or unconscious.

In closing, I return to the words of my mother that open this essay, because she was exhorting Māori to see what was ahead of them, to be far-sighted, wise and expansive. Arapera could not have anticipated the context of diversity, racism and bias that now confronts us, but she was wise enough to know that while we would retain Māori knowledge, especially whakawhanaungatanga, other approaches would also be required to negotiate the world of urban capitalism that would devour us.

Notes

1 Arapera Blank, 'ko taku kumara hei wai-u mo tama', published in *For Someone I Love: A collection of writing by Arapera Blank*, Anton Blank Ltd, 2014
2 https://teara.govt.nz/en/document/3570/the-hunn-report
3 'Pedagogy of the Oppressed': www.litcharts.com/lit/pedagogy-of-the-oppressed/themes/freedom-and-oppression
4 *Puao-Te-Ata-Tu, The Report of the Ministerial Advisory Committee on a Maori Perspective for the Department of Social Welfare*, Wellington, September 1986.
5 www.health.govt.nz/our-work/populations/maori-health/tatau-kahukura-maori-health-statistics/nga-awe-o-te-hauora-socioeconomic-determinants-health/neighbourhood-deprivation
6 Anton Blank, Carla Houkamau & Hautahi Kingi, *Unconscious Bias and Education: A comparative study of Māori and African American Students*, Oranui Press, 2011.
7 www.health.govt.nz/our-work/populations/maori-health/tatau-kahukura-maori-health-statistics/nga-mana-hauora-tutohu-health-status-indicators/suicide-and-intentional-self-harm
8 Blank, Houkamau & Kingi, *Unconscious Bias*.
9 Ibid.

The Landfall Review

Landfall Review Online

www.landfallreview.com

Reviews posted since October 2020
(reviewer's name in brackets)

October 2020

Shape of the Heart by Kevin Ireland (Erik Kennedy)
This is Your Real Name by Elizabeth Morton (Erik Kennedy)
The Wanderer by Ron Riddell (Erik Kennedy)
The Stone Wētā by Octavia Cade (Gina Cole)
Body Politic by Mary Cresswell (Patricia Prime)
Far-Flung by Rhian Gallagher (Patricia Prime)
Michael, I thought you were dead by Michael Fitzsimons (Patricia Prime)
Justice and Race by Oliver Sutherland (Gerry Te Kapa Coates)
Funkhaus by Hinemoana Baker (Vaughan Rapatahana)
Upturned by Kay McKenzie Cooke (Vaughan Rapatahana)
AUP New Poets 6 eds Kemp et al (Vaughan Rapatahana)

November 2020

The Girl from Revolution Road by Ghazaleh Golbakhsh (Helen Watson White)
Enduring Love by Robert McLean (Piet Nieuwland)
How to be Happy Though Human by Kate Camp (Piet Nieuwland)
Yellow Moon by Mary Maringikura (Piet Nieuwland)
New Transgender Blockbusters by Oscar Upperton (Piet Nieuwland)
When We Remember to Breathe by Michelle Powles and Renee Liang (Emma Gattey)
The Stories of Eileen Duggan ed Helen O'Neill (Breton Dukes)
Kalimpong Kids by Jane McCabe (Shana Chandra)

December 2020

This Farming Life by Tim Saunders (Janet Newman)
Every now and then I have another child by Diane Brown (Erik Kennedy)
Unmooring by Bridget Auchmuty (Erik Kennedy)
I Am a Human Being by Jackson Nieuwland (Erik Kennedy)
Sapphic Fragments: Imogen Taylor, essays by Milly Mitchell-Anyon and Joanne Drayton (Robyn Maree Pickens)
Llew Summers by John Newton (Robyn Maree Pickens)
Specimen by Madison Hamill (Emma Gattey)
No Man's Land by A.J. Fitzwater (Cushla McKinney)
Jerningham by Cristina Sanders (Cushla McKinney)

February 2021

Nothing to See by Pip Adam (Chris Else)
A Habit of Writing by Helen Jacobs (Rushi Vyas)
Social Media by Mary Macpherson (Rushi Vyas)
Sinking Lessons by Philip Armstrong (Rushi Vyas)
In the Time of the Manaroans by Miro Bilbrough (Emma Gattey)
Īnangahua Gold by Kathleen Gallagher (Emma Gattey)
Dance Prone by David Coventry (Victor Billot)
Waitangi by Matthew Wright (Gerry Te Kapa Coates)

March 2021

Shining Land by Paula Morris and Haru Sameshima (Sally Blundell)
Me, According to the History of Art by Dick Frizzell (Andrew Paul Wood)
Nouns, Verbs, Etc by Fiona Farrell (Harry Ricketts)
This Pākehā Life by Alison Jones (Wendy Parkins)
Ko Aotearoa Tātou | We Are New Zealand eds Michelle Elvy et al (Gina Cole)

April 2021

Bus Stops on the Moon by Martin Edmond (David Eggleton)
The Strength of Eggshells by Kirsty Powell (Catherine Robertson)
Sprigs by Brannavan Gnanalingam (Catherine Robertson)
Monsters in the Garden eds Elizabeth Knox and David Larsen (Tim Jones)
Letters of Denis Glover ed Sarah Shieff (Robert McLean)
Refocusing Ethnographic Museums by Philipp Schorch et al (Emma Gattey)

Paradoxes, Mysteries and Obsessions

David Eggleton

Ralph Hotere: The dark is light enough by Vincent O'Sullivan (Penguin, 2020), 368pp, $45

The artistic achievement of Ralph Hotere (Te Aupōuri) towers like a great lighthouse above the pure harbour. It's as if he illuminates, with a delicate precision and a sweeping blade of light, New Zealand's brooding darkness, spiritual as well as topographical. Born near Mitimiti, Northland, in 1931 and baptised into the Roman Catholic church as Hone Papita Raukua Hotere, he was an art prodigy almost from the beginning and drew at every opportunity—even with a stick in the sand on the beach near his childhood home, content to watch the waves wash away his efforts. His most remarkable and significant period of artistic production, though, lasted for around forty years between about 1962 and 2002. He died in Dunedin in 2013. His was a busy, restless, crowded existence, as Vincent O'Sullivan tells it in his fascinating 'biographical portrait', which succeeds in synthesising a colourful, gossipy, anecdotal narrative out of the many paradoxes, mysteries and obsessions of this energetic and prolific New Zealand artist's life.

A raft of commentaries and books exists about Hotere's oeuvre and he remains a vital and influential force in the New Zealand cultural matrix, but O'Sullivan's book, with its dextrous assemblage of reminiscences and information, positions Hotere clearly as the pre-eminent artist of the late twentieth century in Aotearoa New Zealand. O'Sullivan does this not so much by emphasising the art historical saga of the heroic artist—the Picasso-like toreador challenging the conventions of art materials, methods and meanings with a cape-twirling flourish—as by telling the story through the various communities that nurtured, nourished and supported Hotere as a person.

Ralph Hotere in this account was first and foremost a Māori, brought up in a whānau and iwi with traditional obligations and relationships. Second, he was steeped in a distinctively French-style Roman Catholicism, instilled among Māori in the Far North by Bishop Jean Baptiste Pompallier (after whom he was named) with the support of what Hotere referred to disparagingly as 'his henchmen'—his priests. So from a young age he was exposed to a spectacle of specific religious rituals and liturgical codes. Third, he was able and self-confident enough to benefit from a benign, if paternalistic, government education policy that sought to promote Māori educators and role models in an era of assimilation. Throughout all this, he was lucky in his timing and fortunate to have benefactors when it counted: Gordon Tovey, the Pākehā arts and crafts visionary who nurtured Hotere's potential; Robert Ellis, the migrant English art lecturer who vouched for Hotere at the crucial 1961 panel meeting to decide who would receive the Association of New Zealand Art Societies travelling scholarship to Britain; and the friendship and inspiration, at Auckland Art Gallery, of Colin McCahon, a primary school arts advisor already intent on becoming a full-time artist, whom Hotere first met in 1953.

As a student at the Dunedin School of Art in the early 1950s, Hotere took part in compulsory military training, but having excellent vision, mechanical aptitude and exceptional mathematical ability, he was one of a select few accepted into the RNZAF. He trained as a pilot at the Taieri aerodrome under World War Two flying ace Wing Commander Checketts. Hotere himself already had a reputation for bravura and a daredevil recklessness, along with anti-authoritarian instincts smouldering beneath a pleasant and well-groomed demeanour. He later said that if he had not been an artist he would have become a pilot: his artworks reveal a fascination with landscapes abstractly seen from above—and with landing strip markings.

But besides this, Hotere remained a good keen bloke, interested for example in sports of all kinds, and a regular pub-goer with an aptitude for fixing cars and DIY repairs. He painted at night after the pub closed, until the small hours, before getting up and going off to work teaching arts and crafts in schools.

Brought up in the blacked-out backblocks of pre-electrification rural New Zealand, Hotere travelled to London in 1961 with his first wife Bet Rameka to study at the Central School of Art. He was exhilarated by his experience of the metropolis. In 1962 he was awarded an artist residency at the Michael Karolyi Memorial arts centre in Vence in the south of France. The Hoteres ended up staying there for three years and used it as a base to visit galleries all over Western Europe. As O'Sullivan establishes, these years exposed Hotere to the significant international art movements of the time and allowed him to grasp the tenets of modernist abstraction from first-hand examples. It was a time of political unrest, too, with many former colonies in Africa and elsewhere—Vietnam for example—seeking independence from European nations: France, Britain and Belgium. Hotere met numerous artists and dissidents and took part in Ban the Bomb marches. It was at this time that he zeroed in on the colour black with all its resonances: blackness was a quality, a value, an emotion.

In 1965 the Hoteres decided to return to Auckland. In 1969 he won the Frances Hodgkins Fellowship and moved to Dunedin with his new partner Maree Morehau—his personal relationships with women were becoming intricate, as O'Sullivan chronicles. The same year, Hotere also produced in a letter to the younger artist, Jeffrey Harris, a kind of personal manifesto: 'I should hate to have other people impose their cruddy bourgeois attitudes on you ... It might be some small consolation to you to learn that after painting for 20 years I've sold maybe a dozen paintings ... I work to please me and I don't give a damn what anyone thinks about it.'

This lack of commercial success was about to change. A 1969 exhibition of black paintings in the Otago Museum foyer was described by the *Otago Daily Times* art critic as 'a tomb of silence, a dignified, profound, heavy silence that reduces the voice to a whisper'. Hotere sold about thirty works at the opening.

By the late 1970s, now married to Cilla McQueen and step-father to her daughter Andrea, Hotere was acknowledged as a leading painter of national significance whose work was beginning to sell well. Many in the arts community shared printmaker Barry Cleavin's estimation that Hotere had 'a divine mark-making facility': whatever he crafted had a distinctive power and beauty as well as an inner conviction. He had also moved from deracinated internationalist abstraction to art-making that emphasised Māoritanga and New Zealand's bicultural identity—while maintaining a commitment to protesting about political oppression, racism and pollution of the environment.

Living at Careys Bay near Port Chalmers, Hotere led the charge against the construction of an aluminium smelter at Aramoana on significant wetlands, with a series of works painted on corrugated iron. In 1981, in response to the National government allowing the Springbok Tour to go ahead, he produced *Black Union Jacks*: dark, angry flags of anti-apartheid protest. By then he was situated as a committed idealist, always metaphorically at the barricades. He was unmistakeably a reflex contrarian, energised by oppressive antagonisms: French nuclear testing in the Pacific, the Gulf War, the 2003 invasion of Iraq. Hotere had the knack of deploying any given nuance of colour to evoke shades of feeling, quivers of attentiveness, with an elegant economy of means: the splash, the drip, the speckling—a mass of dark blotted colours that might suggest both autumn sunlight and an act of remembrance.

Hotere was an artist who had the courage of his convictions, as O'Sullivan's interviewees testify over and over. He conducted himself with a both an indefatigable authenticity and a stylish flair, in all his dealings: in the way he might bargain on the Port Chalmers waterfront for a burnt-out fishing boat hull in order to turn it into an immense work of art; in the way he could drive hell-for-leather through the night on his way back to Dunedin after a late arrival at Christchurch International Airport.

The great Puritan gloom in which Colin McCahon drank and painted with furrowed brow was not Hotere's way. For him life was sensuous, lyrical, passionate. Hotere had a pub dart-thrower's eye, a harbour fisher's perceptiveness, a keen golfer's sense of air and space. If McCahon thumped the table with his big black Bible, Hotere preferred to gently riffle the holy book's gilt-edged pages. Taking a line for a walk as recommended by Paul Klee, he shaped that line of acrylic paint into exquisite arabesques, scrawled on hardboard or canvas, using lines of poetry by Hone Tuwhare, Bill Manhire or Cilla McQueen.

O'Sullivan documents the important women in Hotere's life, from his mother Ana Maria Hotere, to his second wife Cilla McQueen, to his partner Judy Gallie with whom he purchased the Bank of New Zealand building in Port Chalmers, and makes passing mention of his third wife Mary McFarlane in a single sentence, though there he manages to get the date of their wedding wildly wrong.

Besides poets, Hotere worked with a wide circle of artistic collaborators—among them Marian Maguire, Bill Culbert, Russell Moses, Roger Hickin and John Reynolds. In 1998 he collaborated with Mary McFarlane in creating the street sculpture 'Ruaumoko' in central Wellington out of broken Greek columns and bronze lettering, which was commissioned by architect Ian Athfield. By the millennium Hotere was generally acknowledged as New Zealand's most significant artist. The corporate art collector Alan Gibbs flew him to Cuba to see 'failed socialism' close-up; Hotere accepted the trip but not Gibbs' point of view. Hotere was also invited to contribute art for Westpac's national rebranding, and to provide New Zealand cultural ambassador artworks for international art fairs. Yet there was also a public impression of him as untamed: wily and determined, down a foxhole engaged in his own private war with the Establishment, lobbing artworks like fragmentation grenades amid black explosions of paint in order to save his studio, built on an ancient pā site, from container port redevelopment—or else resisting imperialist aggression somewhere in the world.

In August 2001, just before he turned seventy, Hotere suffered a major stroke that caused him serious physical impairment. Thereafter he relied on helpers and carers to produce a much diminished number of artworks. O'Sullivan's narrative becomes somewhat rushed and a bit garbled as it recounts Hotere's final years. This is the result, perhaps, of O'Sullivan only recently returning to complete the last part of the manuscript ahead of publication, having abandoned it around 2010 in frustration at perceived stonewalling from members of the Hotere Foundation Trust, set up between 2003 and 2005 to administer Hotere's legacy. This was about the same time that Ralph Hotere invited Vincent O'Sullivan to write the biography.

Hotere, the swashbuckling cavalier in a Che Guevara beret with his boozing and smoking and fast-lane excesses, always painting like a man in a hurry, painting against the dying of the light: that is the man captured in Vincent O'Sullivan's book. But there's also a sense of him, the art-world superstar, as boxed in at the end, operating at a manic pitch, until suddenly disabled by the stroke that left him more or less in a twilight zone for the remaining decade of his life.

Drink 'til Dead

Janet Newman

The Animals in that Country by Laura Jean McKay (Scribe, 2020), 280pp, $29.99

'Do we want to know what pigs on the way to slaughter are thinking?' asked Australian author Sophie Cunningham at the 31 March 2020 virtual launch of Laura Jean McKay's *The Animals in that Country.* 'No, we don't,' Cunningham answered. But that is what we get in McKay's novel. Battery-farmed pigs are released from a truck on a five-hour-plus trip to the slaughterhouse—this is the Australian outback—because their constant *hello*-ing has unraveled the farmers in the cab. One pig asks, 'Is it / good. What is / it.' It's grass and creeks. We discover that the pigs are not merely fearful; rather, they feel something more terrible and familiar:

> The ones that can walk stretch their legs, for,
>
> **More,**
> **more, more.**
>
> I stand at the top of the truck ramp watching them break into a group trot toward the next paddock. Skin rippling. Hooves carolling. Know that heart-in-your-mouth run. Know exactly what 'more' is ... These pigs are half dead, they're stumbing around, blind, mad, and fucking *hopeful.*

McKay's debut novel upsets not only the conventional power dynamic between people and animals but also the expectations of readers. It is described on its back cover as being about a pandemic, the chief symptom of which is the ability to understand the language of animals. Talking animals! It sounds too corny, but it isn't, because the 'language' is not only verbal but includes sounds, scents and body language—cues from the animal world to which people are generally oblivious.

Hearing the 'voices' of animals sends the human world into chaos. Some people kill or release their pets, some try home lobotomy so they cannot hear them, others swim out to join the whales and drown. Still others relinquish their status as dominators. It is this change in power structure that I take as the central theme of the novel. The pandemic plot is remarkable for its uncanny prescience, including scenarios that once seemed futuristic and are now part of what we call the 'new normal'. Yet it is purely the vehicle to achieve this extraordinary circumstance: human comprehension of the animal world from which flows the novel's brilliance.

In 2021, with ecology at the forefront of much of our thinking, it seems right that a novel about animals talking should foreground their agency, their distinct differences from people and their physical drives. In *The Animals in That Country*—winner of the $100,000 2021 Victorian Prize for Literature—insects say: '**HAS BLOOD**' and '**DRINK 'TIL DEAD. / THE EYES ARE NICE. / AND FULL.**' To craft these monologues, McKay adopts a kind of poetic shorthand, employing bold type and line breaks to distinguish between the 'language' of animals and that of people. She combines the animals' verbal thoughts with an awareness of their body language. Sue the dingo is 'speaking in odours, echoes, noises with random meanings popping out of them. A twitching rear paw. Creaking sounds of welcome in her throat.' At first the words are unintelligible—'**It'll call me and / I'd like / to get a drink of / it.**' But soon this sensory and verbal communication evokes another realm, which some humans come to value.

Central to the success of the plotline is the narrator, Jean, an 'ageing rev-head', alcoholic grandmother, wildlife park guide and wannabe ranger. Her repellent yet attractive character is a credible conveyor of the wild rides McKay takes us on. Through crafted writing, Jean's sometimes repugnant actions are countered by dry humour and a tender heart, as in the following excerpt in which she describes her wayward son:

> When you've birthed someone, you recognise them in any light. He has a way of standing: wonky, but graceful as a dancer ... Barefoot down the warm road I go, unable to keep the smile off my face, even though I know it's best not to encourage him. Because if you give him an inch. My baby. My boy. My little man. Stranger with my skin standing on the other side of the fence ... He's been on the heroin by the sounds of it ... That voice twists my guts, wrings them dry, but it doesn't make any difference to know.

Jean's language portrays the world with unadorned candour—drinking, spewing, pissing, fucking—and dexterous metaphor: 'She gives me a look you might offer a kicked dog'; 'My head like a burrow—I've got to dig myself out of.' Its elemental earthiness permits McKay to intertwine human and animal worlds without straining a reader's suspension of disbelief.

The wildlife park where Jean works is owned by Ange, the mother of Jean's granddaughter, six-year-old Kimberley, who is abducted by her father Lee and taken to the coast to swim with whales. The fast-paced road-chase chronicling Jean's search for her granddaughter drives the plot forward at page-turning speed. It begins about a third of the way into the novel, by which time time all the central human characters are infected with 'zooflu', the viral pandemic. The primary symptom is described as something akin to an acid trip in which enhanced visual, aural and olfactory senses are tuned to the animal world.

Accompanying Jean on the drive south is Sue, a dingo 'camp-mutt-kelpie cross' that Jean found as a pup and reckons she has a special relationship with. Eva Hornung's novel *Dog Boy* (2009) imagines what happens when dogs accept a boy into their pack. McKay imagines what happens when a person accepts a dingo into her life, not as subservient pet but as wild dog with animal agency. In a relationship that flips the power dynamic between human and animal, Sue becomes companion, comforter, guide.

The novel begins with vivid descriptions of Jean's life and character, including her habit of amusing visitors to the park by imagining what the dingoes are saying, thus setting up a contrast between Jean's initial vision and the animal language revealed later. When Sue's foot is stuck in a fence, Jean tugs at the wire to release her. A tourist wants to know what the dingo said:

> The whole lot of them is listening, so I get the mic out. Make my voice high and feathery, like a wild dog tail. 'She said, "Jeanine-girl: you're my best friend."'
>
> They love that.

Ange scolds Jean for 'doing the voices' because 'people who anthropomorphise tend not to read cues, and people who don't read cues are dangerous'. But when the infected Jean comprehends the dingo's thoughts, the results reveal that anthropomorphising animals is not only dangerous but represents a hierarchy of dominance.

McKay ingeniously builds suspense by showing the effects such knowledge has on people, before disclosing what the animals are saying. A man talking to his dog piques Kimberley's curiosity:

> 'I want to talk to a dog,' Kim tells him.
>
> The man straps his mask back on. 'No you don't. My hunting bitch was a tough, mean, fighting machine dog that didn't take shit from nothing. But what she had to say once I knew what it was she was saying—'
>
> 'What'd she say?' Me and Kim at the same time.

By then, I was asking the same question. But it is some time before it is answered. Meanwhile, Jean observes two infected park rangers in the food store where small mammals are bred to feed predators:

> Casey and Liu are out the back, gaping in slack-jawed wonder at the series of bedraggled cages on death row ... The look on Casey's face like the rapture you see on those late night happy-clappy God-botherer shows.

Freshly infected Jean does not immediately comprehend her new sensory awareness. It triggers as she observes mice in the food store:

> Gas rising, not from the pipes, but from their bodies. Not squeaking, screaming. They scream bloody murder, the death of everyone, death in cages and death in the walls ...
> **Run.**
> ... Mice don't talk like that. Mice talk about eating and fucking.

McKay's descriptions of animal signs that were previously undetectable are breathtakingly proficient:

> Round a corner, a bulk of scent nearly knocks me flat. Personal. Someone you don't know waving their rude bits around, then it's gone ... all around me, trails of glowing messages have been laid out overnight. In stench, in calls, in piss, in tracks, in blood, in shit, in sex, in bodies. A big boy wallaroo has rubbed his scent, slick as oil, over the grass at the road edge. It's like running alongside a urinal in a pub.

Jean stuffs flowers in her ears to quieten the animals' voices. Nevertheless, she hears Sue. And now McKay describes what it is like to converse with the nonhuman:

> Just as I skirt around a mossy stump, a voice calls to me like a childhood song:
> **Queen.**
> It rips through my itchy earplugs. I know it. Not Kimberley or Lee or the little things in the tree, but someone so familiar that I skip, God help me, and start toward it.
> **A whiff of**
> **Queen.**
> Slowly tug the flowers out of my ears and squint through the trees. A fly to my left. The stench of the forest, private as an armpit. Sweat pooling cold between my boobs. My special someone calls again.
> **Queen**
> **is here.**
> 'Ange?' Angela won't be calling anyone *Queen*. It's someone else in the bush. I see caramel. Meet with a face so familiar it could be mine. Takes a moment for me to understand it's not human.

It is hardly surprising that McKay was the animal expert presenter on the ABC Listen's *Animal Sound Safari* and that her doctoral thesis focuses on literary animal studies. Born in Victoria, she lectures in creative writing at Massey University. Her first book, *Holiday in Cambodia* (2013), is a collection of short stories. *The Animals in that Country* takes its title from Margaret Atwood's 1968 poem, which contrasts an imagined world where animals are valued with the modern world where they are not.

As McKay reported at the WORD Christchurch Festival last October, her book is like two novels sandwiched together: one about an outback road-chase involving a hard-living, middle-aged woman, the other a dystopian tale of a pandemic, the main symptom of which causes societal collapse. What is admirable is how the excitement of the first and the significance of the second intertwine so that both become part of a whole, where the philosophical questions raised by the power shift between animals and humans are present without overburdening the action of the chase.

Darkly funny, this engrossing novel has a surprisingly affecting end.

Poignancy and Necessity: Posthumous poetry

Siobhan Harvey

No Traveller Returns by Ruth France (Cold Hub Press, 2020), 104pp, $27.50; **Wanting to Tell You Everything** by Elizabeth Brooke-Carr (Caselberg Press, 2020), 66pp, $25; **The Needles of the Marram Grass** by W.S. Broughton (SwampThing, 2019), 130pp, $25

The ease with which we forget or cast aside writers after their deaths, particularly those identifying as women, non-Pākehā and non-hetero-normative, is a problem with a long history. For centuries, authors around the world and their bodies of work have been lost to subsequent generations.

No Traveller Returns by Ruth France, *Wanting to Tell You Everything* by Elizabeth Brooke-Carr and *The Needles of the Marram Grass* by W.S. Broughton are three posthumously published New Zealand collections. The poetry within their covers illustrates the way that powerful work endures beyond an author's passing. These books are potential prompts to us to rethink how we save and savour contemporary literature so that future generations have access to it.

It's always a pleasure to discover a consummate poet and their breathtaking work. In the case of Ruth France, the delight in engaging with the selection of poems assembled in *No Traveller Returns* is enhanced by their extensive number and the cogent introduction by Christchurch poet and literary critic Robert McLean. There are nearly fifty poems showcased in the book. These are chosen from the two collections France published in her lifetime under the pseudonym Paul Henderson—*Unwilling Pilgrim* (Caxton Press, 1955) and *The Halting Place* (Caxton Press, 1961) —as well as from the titular unpublished book of verse.

France's poems are interesting because of their complexity. So often in the past women writers have been dismissed for their singularity of focus and subject: the domestic. Those New Zealand women poets of the 1930s–50s—like Hyde and Mackay—whose work too often broke this socially engineering perception, did so in the face of distrust and sneering from members of a male-dominated literati. As in France's award-winning novels *The Race* (1958) and *Ice Cold River* (1961), the layers and nuances to the work in *No Traveller Returns* pulls the reader into an exploration of double meanings, lyrical language and shifts in subject matter. With its opening lines focused on deconstructing the notion that personhood is composed of two selves, the first poem, 'Unwilling Pilgrim', is evidence of this:

> If there were no second self he would sit
>
> Comfortably at home among the cabbages,
> And persuade himself that to tend the puny
> ravages
> Of butterfly, and drought upon the lawn, and
> spot
>
> In espaliered peaches, would enclose his
> soul …

The idea that life is more knotted than its portrayals in religion, politics, the economy and even the arts is a message threaded through most of the early poems in *No Traveller Returns*. The schmaltz of love songs is exposed in 'The Young Legend', for instance. The migrant dream of a better future to be found in Aotearoa is condemned in 'The Ghost Ships'.

Instead, France's work reminds us that life is multifaceted; only by accepting this and the intricate layers that compose our personality will we find self-acceptance and value in existence. Such ideas are inherited and developed by the verses from the book's other sections, 'The Halting Place' and 'No Traveller Returns'. Here, in poems such as 'Elegy', 'Suburb at Night' and 'I Think of Those', life isn't harmonious but rather is a complicated intersection of the good, the bad and the mundane. Death; our intricate connection to others; the hollowness of suburban living; the power and profundity of nature: these things triumph in the messages layered into France's poems.

No Traveller Returns is a powerful and surprisingly modern collection. Its topics and themes might have been forged in the 1950s and 60s but they resound down the decades and remain prescient today. I applaud Cold Hub Press and Robert McLean for collecting and analysing

Ruth France's work. Too long overlooked, France and her compelling work are given the attention they rightfully deserve in this book of selected poems.

The first two poems in Elizabeth Brooke-Carr's *Wanting to Tell You Everything* occur around the kitchen table. Proof that women poets are absorbed by the domestic space? Not at all. Rather, this setting is an arena for deeper interrogation. In the introductory poem 'Upright', for instance, an entire era of familial interaction unfolds, while in the next verse, 'Many Breakfasts Since', the minutiae of a marriage is unpicked.

What follows are poems focused on what women poets often write about so well (the very issues for which, historically, they've been dismissed and misunderstood): the significance found in details and small exchanges, in garden plots and garden fences, and in raising children and communing with grandchildren.

As in France's *No Traveller Returns*, so with Brooke-Carr's poetry: the subjects are only part of the rich poetic interplay on the page. For both poets, the other part of the lyrical exchange is craft. Both collections prove their authors are skilled technical practitioners. Where *Wanting to Tell You Everything* is concerned, for instance, the varied forms—free verse, prose-poem—are tightly knit and symphonic. Poetic concision requires an expert hand, eye and tongue, and poems such as 'Memory of Snow' prove Brooke-Carr possessed all the necessary faculties for literary success. This is a poem which, upon first and subsequent readings, offers echoes of the work of that greatly underrated poet Jane Kenyon, whose melodic spirituality is present also in Brooke-Carr's lines, such as:

> From the wall beside the window
> my bearded brother stares down,
> shadow cast across his face. Snow,
> we called him. Blond hair slicked back,
> blue eyes, corner-crinkled, laughing into
> mine ...

The lines are consistent in their length and syllabic music as well as in their restraint. Nothing here shouts of loss; instead, bereavement is offered with precision in such carefully chosen elements as the shadow, the brother's nickname and his blue eyes.

Reading Brooke-Carr reminds us of the importance of poetry and, as this is her first and only collection, of not letting the work of those poets who are no longer alive slip into obscurity.

Talk of craft and poetic dexterity makes for an excellent segue into W.S. Broughton's posthumous collection, *The Needles of the Marram Grass*. Broughton was best known for his selfless and persuasive championing of other writers' work. For over four decades he taught New Zealand literature at Massey University and occasionally found his poems published in fine literary journals like *Evergreen Review* (US). On the strength of *The Needles of the Marram Grass*, this reviewer is left feeling that Broughton deserved to focus as much on his own output as that of others.

Collectively, the poems possess a painterly quality. Imagery—particularly that evoking the innumerable luscious landscapes of Aotearoa—acts as core subject matter again and again; the poems 'A Poem to Colin McCahon—Kahuterawa Valley', 'Recollections—Lyttelton Harbour' and 'Triptych' deserve particular praise.

'Triptych', for instance, is so crisp in its descriptions that they come immediately alive in the mind:

> I kissed my love three times
>
> once in the night with the hoar haze
> crinkling the stars, making them moist
> in the dry sky, while the houses
> and the streets lay pale in the black
>
> and black in the pale light of the
> winter's breathing ...

Here is a nightscape so worthy of McCahon, Angus or Bensemann it might almost be framed. The same kind of visual and aesthetic interaction between the pictorial and poetic is evident in 'A Poem for Colin McCahon—Kahuterawa Valley'. In the nine lines of this work, Broughton forges an unequivocal chemistry between canvas, consciousness and poetic craft, as evidenced by this section:

> Because I've seen your paintings,
> clean, cold, sharp, loving,
> it follows that I see these hills.
> Each time the car wheel turns
> —the road following—my windscreen
>   frames
> a new vision, three, four lines
> clean, cold green ...

The sections of *The Needles of the Marram Grass* offer elements from three unpublished collections crafted during Broughton's lifetime. Though they didn't see the light of day as individual books, their assemblage in this recent publication offers their own triptych of a poet and his work deserving of wider local recognition.

There's a poignancy—and necessity—in reading these three posthumous publications. At a time when there's a welcome abundance of new books by local authors being published, particularly poetry collections, it's noticeable to this reviewer how the work of talented writers of the past like France, Brooke-Carr and Broughton is not being remembered, anthologised and celebrated as widely and thoroughly as is warranted. In part, these books restore some of this cultural neglect. More importantly, of course, they showcase the poetry, craft and storytelling of three amazing and highly gifted New Zealand poets.

History So Close It Wounds

Helen Watson White

Te Papa to Berlin: The making of two museums by Ken Gorbey (Otago University Press, 2020), 245pp, $39.95

'Storytelling is perhaps the most potent of humanising forces,' writes Ken Gorbey, echoing the great Italian Jewish humanist Primo Levi. From a civic job in Hamilton merging the city's art gallery and Waikato Museum into one building, and after heading Wellington's project team for the Museum of New Zealand Te Papa Tongawera, likewise a merger of New Zealand's National Museum and National Art Gallery, Gorbey moved to Berlin to rescue the foundering Jewish Museum Berlin (JMB). While it already had a building of dramatic and unique design, there was no plan for projects to fill it. In all three places the focus became storytelling, with the development of the first two institutions strongly supported by Māori leaders and using foundational Māori concepts of identity and mana.

The Aotearoa New Zealand part of Gorbey's memoir—a story about stories—makes up only one-third of the volume, yet the effects of his experience of working with Māori in exposing the 'dark' side of our national history are felt throughout the remaining two-thirds, beginning with Chapter 7, entitled 'What's the Boy from Maungatautari Doing Here [in Berlin]?' That question was doubtless asked by the existing staff of the JMB as well as by New Zealanders, and indeed prospective readers of this book. It is quite a triumph that Gorbey has been able to ease us through the transitions with humour and humility, so that the development of Germany's national Jewish museum along the lines of Te Papa becomes understandable and 'right'.

The JMB was, like Te Papa, intended to represent fully the shameless treatment of minorities, but it was to do much more than that. The new Jewish national museum was charged with presenting not just the history of the Holocaust, but the whole 2000-year story of Jews in Germany, just as Te Papa/Our Place was to represent nothing less than the history of the land and people(s) of Aotearoa: Pacific voyages in waves of immigration; so-called 'high art' along with functional design; individual stories alongside cultural narratives.

A focus on storytelling meant that, for both Waikato and Te Papa, a building uniting the art gallery and museum would not be considered in the conventional way as just a home for historic collections. At the JMB, there was no vision for the new building—an extension of the baroque Kollegienhaus (home of the old Berlin City Museum)—beyond a vague expectation that it would house inanimate objects and displays of some kind.

Daniel Libeskind's design for the new JMB, constructed on war-smashed wasteland in former East Berlin was, for Gorbey, 'like nothing we had seen before'. Large, coldly metallic—brutal, even—it looked like some sort of industrial structure, but skewed out of normal proportions. Its floormap was the crazy diagonal shape of a lightning bolt writ large. Its vertical elevation was also jagged; nothing was familiar, nothing was square, and its forbidding front face was slashed with narrow windows at seemingly random angles. Gorbey called them 'terminal wounds'.

The fact that it was empty, however, made it open to possibilities, writes Gorbey: 'Less than a year since its completion, the building was already timeless, speaking as much of the Thirty Years' War as Daniel's take on the Holocaust, a set waiting for Bertolt Brecht to stage *Mother Courage and her Children*.' Gorbey often speaks of a museum space, enlivened by exhibitions, as a form of 'magical' theatre.

The author was first invited to Berlin in 1999 as part of a review team to assess, in the words of JMB director Michael Blumenthal, 'where we're at'. From the first day this proved an agonizing experience. The staff had prepared a single model of a possible (static) exhibition, which meant there was little to assess. Gorbey took the director aside, hardly needing to explain to this Jewish former child-refugee, now a successful New York businessman, how much was at stake: 'We could not disappoint. The German-Jewish story, and the building, already an architectural masterwork, deserved better.'

The review was quickly reconvened as a workshop, with the visiting team imagining themselves as colleagues. Jim Volkert (at the time leading Washington's National Museum of the American Indian project) urged the resident staff to pull back and look at the museum space as a whole, asking how the storytelling might be influenced by its 'bizarre' architectural environment. Gorbey, in remembering that day, reflects on this theme:

> Every other museum I had dealt with had either traditional galleries of rectangular shape or, as in Te Papa, vast open volumes in which we could build what we wanted. But the long string of twisting spaces that made Libeskind's building was quite different. It was unrelentingly linear. Such a layout … gives direction to visitors as they move from the first experience to the second … and so on. But visitors also like to make their own decisions about what to see and where to go next. This creates a real quandary for the experience developer. If contained and herded, visitors can rebel; if the exhibitions are too unstructured they will lose their way. In both cases they might defect, the official term for giving up and leaving in bad humour.

The review team's role, as Gorbey saw it, was to ask some fundamental questions: 'Why should visitors come to the Jewish Museum Berlin? What will they take from their visit? Why should the government fund us? What is the sense of purpose that guides the stories you tell?'

While the team's conclusions were almost entirely negative, Blumenthal was so impressed with Gorbey's clear-sightedness that he hired him on the spot to build a future for the JMB that had yet to be envisaged. He said, 'I need the right person to see this museum through to opening'—in under two years.

This was a huge challenge for Gorbey and later for Wellington writer Nigel Cox, the one staff member he was allowed to bring from the Te Papa project team. From the first, there was the problem outlined by Michael Blumenthal in his Foreword: 'The Nazis had destroyed not only Jewish life in Germany, but also its symbols and artefacts, so what was there to exhibit?'

This underlying concern was one of the principles addressed in 'intensive' Friday conversations between Gorbey and a colleague, fellow-anthropologist Dr Vera Bendt. The very absence of what used to be considered museum material became a major theme, honoured with its own name: 'missingness'. Alongside project planning meetings, such personal conversations were vital, on multiple fronts, for a New Zealander speaking no German, who came to sense deeply the 'angst that formed much of the German character. History so close it wounds. Memories like salt in those wounds.'

History, of course, kept happening within the compass of this book, the New York twin-towers outrage assaulting the senses of an exhausted Berlin team who, having celebrated the JMB's official grand opening on 9 September, were preparing for its unveiling to the public on 11 September 2001.

Gorbey's memoir, therefore, does not stop with the culmination of twenty-three months' work centred on Libeskind's building. Much travelled in the course of his museum-oriented career, he extends his observations on anti-Semitism and nationalism to a broader exploration of values in recent history and in the development of Germany's newly united liberal democracy.

Throughout the book, personal reflection brings unexpected rewards for the reader. After the 'desperation' of management wars at Te Papa, and despite the struggle to apply South Pacific values in a conservative European context, Gorbey admits moments of joy that come with building deep friendships that will outlast his Berlin time. At the lowest point of all, when the effects of 9/11 were being felt all around the world, he celebrated, with partner Susan Foster, the birth of triplets to his daughter Susi and son-in-law Erwan in London; he includes a photo taken some weeks later, of the infants with their father and first-time grandfather.

There are two sections of such candid photos, their placement often making an ironic point. Facing this domestic photo, for instance, is an image of artist Menashe Kadishman's *Shalechet/Falling Leaves*: thousands of screaming deathmasks that are stepped on by visitors traversing JMB's Main Void. Turn the page and you are met by grim Soviet-era statuary photographed on a trip to Moscow. The book (and the JMB) are,

Gorbey insists, about *life*, in its sometimes chaotic variety.

One might expect that a memoir of this kind could be self-absorbed or, at worst, self-serving. There is no trace of this, for the author includes a wide circle of collaborators in both the process and the success of his envisioning, and this rings true. Having visited both Te Papa and the JMB with young relatives, I can attest to the power of these truly inclusive institutions to move people in ways they would not otherwise be moved.

The commitment to change brought by the makers of Te Papa means that it, too, continues to evolve, and the principles that went into its making are alive and well on the other side of the world. When you read of Gorbey's two museums side by side, and of the millions who have enjoyed them (two million in Te Papa's first year), you'd be hard-pressed to think of reasons why they should not have been developed in the way that they have.

No Light in the Woods

Rachel O'Connor

Remote Sympathy by Catherine Chidgey (Victoria University Press, 2020), 528pp, $35

Even in the idle days of early January I struggled to finish Catherine Chidgey's *Remote Sympathy*. It is 528 pages long, and I was unable to read it at night; sleep afterwards proved impossible. The novel is set almost entirely in Buchenwald, one of Germany's largest and most infamous concentration camps of the Second World War. Accordingly, even the most ignorant reader must know they will enter a world of unmitigated horror. The early optimism offered by protagonist Doktor Lenard Weber's joyful marriage to Jewess Anna, and his invention of the Sympathetic Vitaliser, a machine he hopes will cure cancer through electrotherapy, is necessarily short-lived. There can be no happy ending to a Holocaust story, even if it is fiction, even if the hero, by some miracle, survives.

In 1930s Frankfurt the toxic fog of the Third Reich is rising inexorably. When Weber's medical career becomes compromised by his marriage to Anna and by his own 'difficult ancestry', the perceived 'taint' of Jewish blood uncovered in his family tree, the couple divorce and Anna enters a 'safer' marriage of convenience. It does not save them. Rules tighten further, transportations begin, and in 1943 Anna and daughter Lotte are deported, perhaps to Theresienstadt; and Weber, a 'Mischling' now classified as a political enemy of the Reich, is imprisoned at Buchenwald. In his letters to Lotte, written from Frankfurt in 1946, we receive his account, pragmatic, almost dispassionate in tone, of the human hell that he witnesses and endures therein.

The imaginary diary of Greta, youthful wife of SS Sturmbannführer Dietrich Hahn, the camp's ambitious administrator who takes up office in the year of Weber's arrival, forms the second voice of the narrative. Out of her depth in the farcically extravagant community of the Reich's local rulers, Greta senses but never directly confronts the horrors that lie on the other side of the forest. Under the tutelage of Emmi Wolff, wife of the prison compound commander, Greta learns to navigate and exploit their life of parasitic luxury, but her unease persists. Sour smoke from the camp's chimney infuses the air, periodic gunshots signal that another prisoner has been 'shot while attempting to escape', and the citizens of nearby Weimar avoid eye contact with her on her excursions to the town. Her tentative questions receive only glib answers, however, and truth remains out of sight beyond the trees.

The presence of the captive masses is sublimated instead through an unnerving parade of constricted animals: limp-necked poultry are strung up in the cellar, the falconry keeps tethered birds of prey, the residents' private zoo boasts caged monkeys and bears, and rabbits crammed in a hutch are produced for the children's entertainment. Most powerful among these metaphoric creatures is the animal kingdom that Sturmbannführer Hahn carves from oak, two by two, for their small son Karl-Heinz. Without an ark to shelter them, or a Noah to lead them, these wooden animals are moved about the house at Karl-Heinz's whim, jammed into the carriages of his toy railway, balanced precariously on the edges of stairs or filling bathtubs. When the boy is compelled to sacrifice a tiger as punishment for an act of cruelty, he surrenders one of the pair and saves the other. Yet there is barely a difference between them, no discernible distinction to determine why one is retained while the other is tossed into the fire. Survival is arbitrary, merely a matter of chance.

The third narrative voice, sharing the private reflections of one thousand citizens of Weimar, is perhaps the most chilling, and timely, in its veracity. Beneath the bourgeois chatter and litany of complaint, a solid, impermeable layer of complicity, delusion and denial is revealed, in which misinformation proliferates like bacteria, culpability dissolves, and the individual voices of humanity and reason are stomped into silence. Yet we wish to believe that at least some of them are truly ignorant of the atrocities that take place on their doorstep. They are, after all, just ordinary people.

Sturmbannführer Hahn delivers the fourth narrative thread, in recordings made by an unidentified interviewer in 1956. Most directly involved, of all the narrators, with the actuality of torture, starvation and death that constitute the daily business of the camp, his character cannot hope to engage a reader's sympathy; we know too much, and even the most accomplished author cannot render the inhuman human. Yet against all odds, Hahn becomes real. Desperate for professional and peer recognition, beset with personal insecurities and overwhelmed by the burgeoning administrative challenges of the camp, he worries constantly about his performance. In a line of defence made commonplace in the trials that followed the war, Hahn details for his listener the systems and regulations by which he was bound, the shortages and shifting parameters that rendered him powerless to improve the rations or conditions of prisoners, the economies he was forced to exercise to meet the targets imposed on him. Among the barrage of calculations and statistics that Hahn recounts, the mounting tally of corpses—by war's end too many even to bury or burn—becomes just one more number that is beyond his control.

In his operational account of the workings of the nightmare that was Buchenwald, Hahn clearly speaks with the brash voice of the Reich. So entirely invested is he in the doctrine of his party, and in the security and prestige it promises him, that those interred in the camp retain no more humanity for him than the collection of gold teeth he hoards in a chocolate box. Yet he loves his wife and child, and when Greta develops cancer he risks all that he has gained to bring Weber to their home, bribing him to reconstruct his Sympathetic Vitaliser machine and administer its treatments. Each guilty of a selfish failure to act, when they could have, to save their wives, the two men now form a grim, unequal alliance, observing the battle within Greta's frail body while around them the Reich crumples and implodes in the final days of the war.

In his opening letters to Lotte, Weber informs her that his story will contain three miracles. While the first transpires to be no more than fortuitous coincidence, and the second a temporary and insubstantial reprieve, the third miracle proves to be real, a flickering afterthought of hope that can do little to dispel the cumulative darkness of the novel. In reality, of course, there were no miracles. Those who had been marked to perish and yet survived the Holocaust did so by chance, or through the will and courage of other humans who stepped into the path of fate and pulled them from under the oncoming wheels of the machine. Albert Bourla, CEO of Pfizer, the pharmaceuticals company now leading the battle to save the world's people with its Covid-19 vaccine, marked International Holocaust Remembrance Day in 2021 by sharing the story of his own parents. Sephardic Jews from Thessaloniki, Greece, the couple were among only four percent of the city's Jewish population of 50,000 to survive. That they lived was due to the courage, altruism and quick thinking of others, Christians and Jews, who acted without hesitation when the opportunity arose to offer aid. Such human interventions, those individual small acts that tip the scale from death to life, are the stuff of any great war story. They offer the reader a lighted candle and the rush of relief that accompanies the evidence of enduring good even as we are confronted with the terrible scale of our human capacity for evil.

Remote Sympathy extends no such relief. There is no real redemption even for those who survive this story; the crushing weight of its irrefutability renders everything dark. It is not, then, a book I could enjoy, yet I found much to admire within it. On occasion the persistent revelations of research drown out the narrative, and we teeter on the tightrope strung between fiction and fact, but Chidgey's elegant, rhythmic prose is expertly controlled, and the heavy slabs of history are interleaved with delicate, polished imagery steeped in subtle menace. The creeping shifts in civil liberties, attitudes and ambitions, and the pressure and paranoia that spread as Hitler's Reich gains momentum, are drawn with shrewd, oblique strokes. The settings and rituals of both prison and privileged life are made original by vivid sensory detail. The endless lists—of food, of clothing, of photographs, of fixtures, of songs and rules and punishments and ways to die—support the body of the narrative like so many stacked bones. It is a brilliant and terrible book, one that I might wish I could unread, and yet am grateful I cannot.

Adapt or Die, cont'd from page 9

Within that time the toll taken environmentally and socially will be both devastating and largely irreversible. The facts and figures presented by the scientific quorum are deafening in their message; the communities and unique environment of this nation are at risk. Mitigation is not enough—it is not a restorative magic wand. It needs to be partnered with equally detailed, inclusive adaptation policy. The alternative to reaching the set 2050 emissions targets will be evolving amphibious lungs.

Sources

Ministry for the Environment Manatū Mo Te Taiao, 'Environment Aotearoa 2019': www.mfe.govt.nz/environment-aotearoa-2019

Otago Regional Council: www.orc.govt.nz/

The Intergovernmental Panel on Climate Change: www.ipcc.ch/

United Nations Climate Change: https://unfccc.int/

World Meteorological Organization: https://public.wmo.int/en

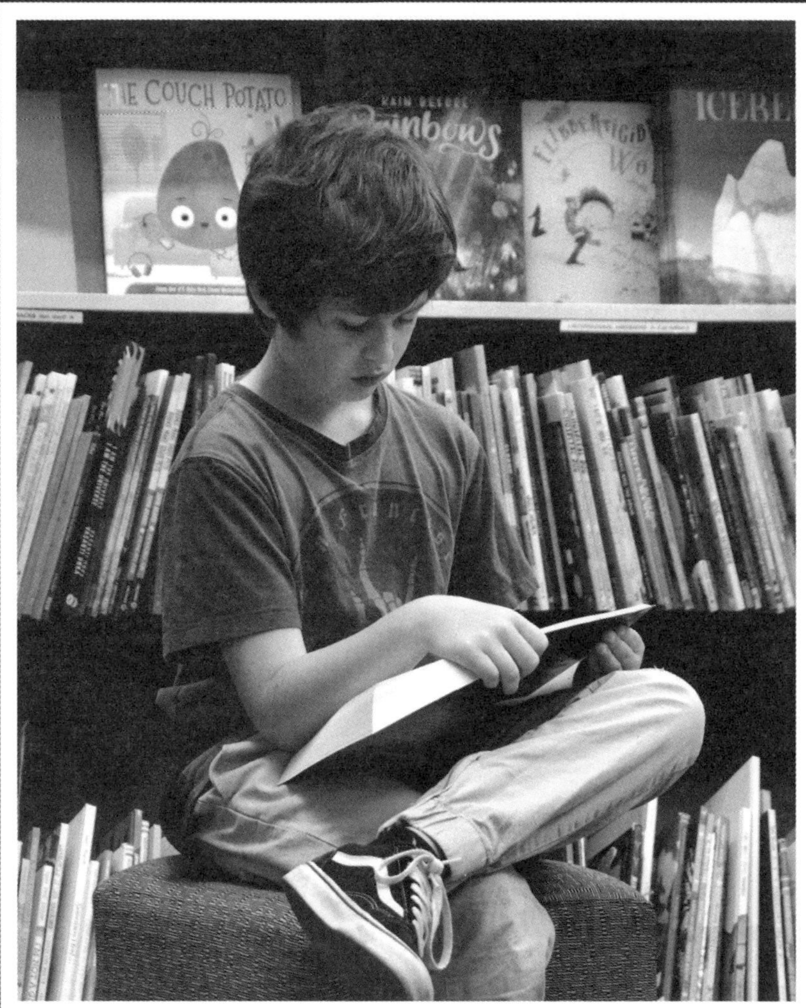

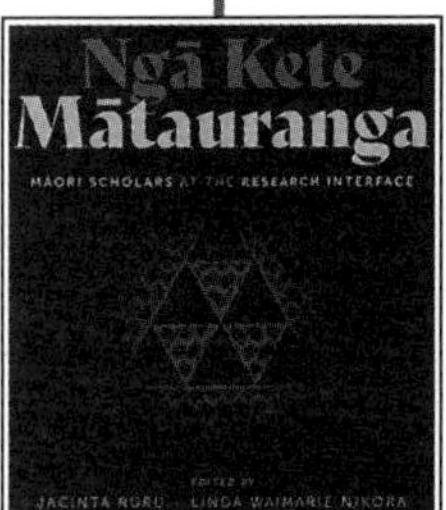

Ngā Kete
Mātauranga
MĀORI SCHOLARS AT THE RESEARCH INTERFACE
JACINTA RURU · LINDA WAIMARIE NIKORA

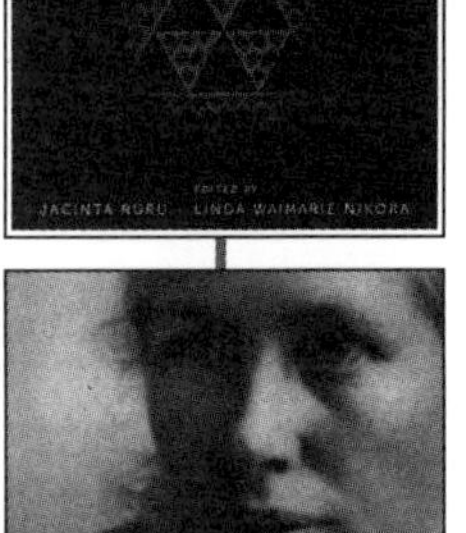

Kate
Edger
THE LIFE OF A
PIONEERING FEMINIST
Diana Morrow

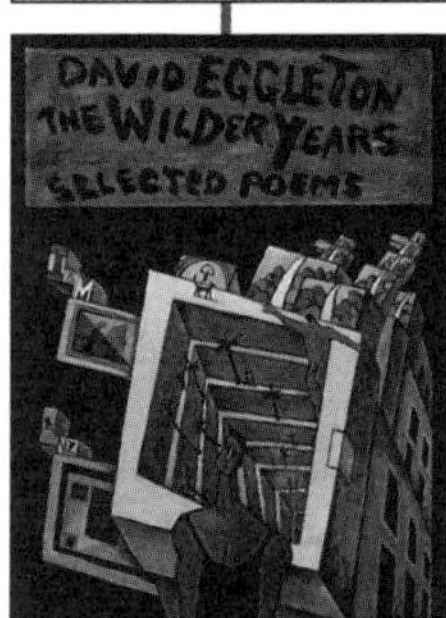

DAVID EGGLETON
THE WILDER YEARS
SELECTED POEMS

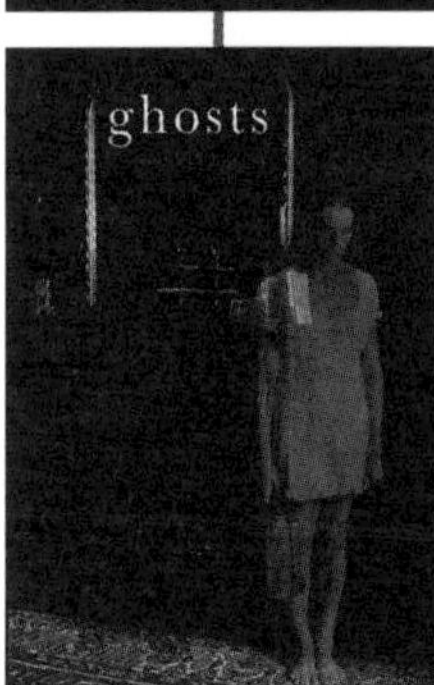

ghosts

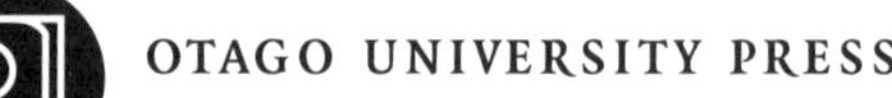

OTAGO UNIVERSITY PRESS
From good booksellers or www.otago.ac.nz/press

CONTRIBUTORS

Johanna Aitchison has published three volumes of poetry, including *Miss Dust* (Seraph Press, 2015) and *a long girl ago* (Victoria University Press, 2007). Her poetry has appeared in *Sport*, *Landfall* and *Turbine|Kapohau*.

Philip Armstrong teaches literature and creative writing at the University of Canterbury. His recent collection of poems, *Sinking Lessons* (Otago University Press, 2020), won the 2019 Kathleen Grattan Award.

Kirsty Baker is an art historian and writer based in Te Whanganui-a-Tara. Her research is informed by the interlinked nature of the political and the creative. She has written for *Art New Zealand*, *Pantograph Punch*, *Artist Profile* and *Art and Australia*, among other publications.

Rebecca Ball is a teacher based in Christchurch. She has had poems published in *English in Aotearoa* and *London Grip*, as well as a narrative study guide, *BA: An insider's guide* (Auckland University Press, 2012).

David Beach lives in Wellington. He has written six books of sonnets, most recently *Laboratory Hill* (self-published, 2019).

Dunedin-based **Peter Belton** is a visual artist with particular interest in writing about the stories of other artists' situations and, in another body of work, impressions recalled from childhood.

Claire Beynon is a Dunedin-based artist, writer and interdisciplinary researcher. In addition to her solo practice, she works collaboratively on a diverse range of projects with fellow artists, writers, scientists and musicians in New Zealand and abroad.

Anton Blank (Ngāti Porou, Ngāti Kahungunu) has an extensive history in social work, communications, Māori development, public health and literature. Anton is also the editor and founder of the Māori literary journal *Ora Nui*.

Diana Bridge's seventh collection of poems, *Two or more islands*, was published by Otago University Press (2019), and *At the Eastern Window: Three essays* appeared in 2020.

Owen Bullock has published a novella, three collections of poetry and five books of haiku, the most recent being *Summer Haiku* and *Work & Play* (Recent Work Press, 2019 and 2017). He teaches creative writing at the University of Canberra, and his website for research into poetry and process can be found at https://poetry-in-process.com/

Stephanie Burt is a professor of English at Harvard and has also taught at the University of Canterbury in Christchurch and Macalester College in St Paul. Her most recent books include *After Callimachus* (Princeton University Press, 2020) and *Don't Read Poetry: A book about how to read poems* (Basic, 2019).

Cadence Chung is a student at Wellington High School. She first started writing poetry during a particularly boring maths lesson when she was nine, and hasn't stopped since. She enjoys antique stores and classic literature and tries her best to be an Edwardian dandy.

Ruth Corkill is a poet from Aotearoa and a graduate of the Iowa Writers Workshop MFA programme. Her work has appeared in *The Feminist Wire*, *Landfall*, *Poetry NZ*, *New Welsh Review*, *Wasafiri* and *The Moth*. She is currently pursuing a PhD in physics at the University of Stuttgart and was part of a 2019 Modern Languages Association symposium panel on Contemporary Physics Poetry.

Mary Cresswell lives on the Kāpiti Coast. Her latest book, *Body Politic* (The Cuba Press, 2020), includes nature poems for nature in crisis.

Majella Cullinane writes poetry, fiction and essays. Otago University Press published her second poetry collection *Whisper of a Crow's Wing* in 2018. She was awarded a Copyright Licensing NZ grant in 2019, and recently received a Creative NZ Arts grant to work on her third collection of poetry.

Alison Denham's work has appeared in poetry journals and anthologies in New Zealand, the UK and the US. In 2014 her second collection of poems, *Raspberry Money*, was published by Sudden Valley Press for the Canterbury Poets Collective.

Murray Edmond is the editor of *Ka Mate Ka Ora* (www.nzepc.auckland.ac.nz/kmko/). His published work includes *Back Before You Know* (Compound Press, 2019) and *Strait Men and Other Tales* (Steele Roberts, 2015). *Time to Make a Song and Dance: Cultural revolt in Auckland in the 1960s* is forthcoming from Atuanui Press.

Ben Egerton is a Wellington poet and teaches in the Faculty of Education at Victoria University of Wellington. Ben's poetry, and his writing about poetry, have been published in New Zealand and overseas.

David Eggleton is a writer, poet and reviewer based in Ōtepoti/Dunedin, and is the Aotearoa New Zealand Poet Laureate 2019–2022.

Hetty Finney Waters is a year twelve student at Otago Girls' High School. Her passions include public speaking, literature and activism on issues such as climate change and human rights.

Alison Glenny's collection of prose poems *The Farewell Tourist* was published by Otago University Press in 2018, having won the Kathleen Grattan Poetry Award in 2017. A chapbook, *Bird Collector*, is being published by Compound Press in 2021.

Jordan Hamel is the 2018 NZ Poetry Slam champion. He is also the co-editor of *Stasis Journal* and co-editor of a forthcoming anthology of climate change poetry from Auckland

University Press. He is a 2021 Michael King writer-in-residence and his work has been published in *The Spinoff*, *Newsroom*, *Sport Poetry NZ*, *Landfall* and elsewhere.

Trisha Hanifin has a master's degree in creative writing from Auckland University of Technology. Her flash fiction has been published in various journals and anthologies including *Flash Frontier*, *Headland*, *Fresh Ink* and *Bonsai: Best small stories from Aotearoa New Zealand* (Canterbury University Press, 2018).

Michael Harlow has published thirteen books of poetry, the latest being *The Moon in a Bowl of Water* (Otago University Press, 2018). He received the Prime Minister's Award for Literary Achievement in Poetry 2018. He lives and works in Central Otago as a poet, editor, essayist and Jungian therapist.

Siobhan Harvey is the author of five books, including the 2013 Kathleen Grattan Poetry Award-winning collection *Cloudboy* (Otago University Press, 2014) and, as editor, *Essential New Zealand Poems* (Godwit, 2014). *Ghosts* is forthcoming from Otago University Press.

Christchurch-based **Amy Head** has written a short-story collection *Tough* (2013) and a novel *Rotoroa* (2018), both published by Victoria University Press.

Chris Holdaway is a poet and bookmaker from Te Tai Tokerau/Northland. He directs Compound Press in Auckland, and his book *Gorse Poems* is forthcoming from Titus Books. His poetry has appeared in numerous publications including *Cordite*, *Poetry NZ*, *Shearsman* and *Western Humanities Review*, and his prose in *Jacket2* and *Ka Mate Ka Ora*.

Lily Holloway is a queer postgraduate English student who probably wants to be your pen pal. Her work is forthcoming in *AUP New Poets 8*, and you can also find her writing at lilyholloway.co.nz.

Claudia Jardine is a recent returnee to Ōtautahi and holds a Master of Arts in classics. A selection of her poetry was published in *AUP New Poets 7* alongside the work of Rhys Feeney and Ria Masae (Auckland University Press, 2020). More of her work can be found in *Starling*, *Sport*, *Stasis* and on her bandcamp webpage.

J. Wiremu Kane (Ngāpuhi) lives and writes on the ancestral lands of Ngāti Hei and Ngāti Maru. His novels and short stories seek to expose the gaping, unhealed wound colonisation has wrought on this whenua and its people.

Erik Kennedy is the author of *There's No Place Like the Internet in Springtime* (Victoria University Press, 2018) and co-editor of an anthology of climate change poetry from Aotearoa New Zealand and the Pacific, due out in 2021 from Auckland University Press.

Brent Kininmont's poems can be found online and in his collection *Thuds Underneath* (Victoria University Press, 2015).

Lyndsey Knight makes textile art and writes short stories, poetry and flash fiction, engaging in all her art practices with equal enthusiasm. She was born in Christchurch and lives in Auckland.

Sarah Lawrence is a second-year student at Victoria University. She likes sparrows, Tchaikovsky and the colour yellow. She hates regulation school shoes and people who are rude to waiters.

Wen-Juenn Lee uses her writing to explore concepts of home—a word that leaks. She currently serves as a poetry editor at *Voiceworks*. Her writing has appeared in *Scum Mag*, *Going Down Swinging*, *Landfall* and other places.

Wes Lee lives in Paekakariki. Her latest poetry collection is *By the Lapels* (Steele Roberts, 2019). Her work has appeared in *Best New Zealand Poems*, *Westerly*, *Magma*, *The Stinging Fly*, *Abridged* and *Australian Poetry Journal*, among others. She was awarded the Poetry New Zealand Prize 2019.

Talia Marshall (Ngāti Kuia/Rangitāne o Wairau/Ngāti Rārua/Ngāti Takihiku) is a Dunedin-based writer who is currently working on a book of essays tentatively titled 'Boy Crazy' and a poetry collection with the equally tentative title of 'Bad Apple'.

Ria Masae is a writer, spoken-word poet and librarian of Samoan descent, and was born and raised in Tāmaki Makaurau. Her work has been published in literary outlets such as *Landfall*, *takahē*, *Circulo de Poesia* and *Best New Zealand Poems 2017*. A collection of her poetry is published in *AUP New Poets 7* (Auckland University Press, 2020).

Ewan McDougall has had ninety solo exhibitions in New Zealand, and his work has been shown in London, Valencia, Cremona, New York and Sydney. His paintings are held in many public collections and have been described as psychedelic cave art.

Caoimhe McKeogh has an MA in creative writing from Victoria University of Wellington. Her poetry and prose have been widely published in Australia and New Zealand, including in *Overland*, *Turbine|Kapohau*, *Starling*, *Cordite*, *Meniscus* and *Mimicry*. She is a member of the editorial team at *Headland Journal*.

James McNaughton has published two poetry collections and, more recently, two novels with Victoria University Press: *New Hokkaido* (2015) and *Star Sailors* (2017).

Zoë Meager is from Ōtautahi. Her work has appeared abroad in publications including *Granta* and *Overland*, and locally in *Landfall*, *Mayhem*, *Turbine|Kapohau* and *Bonsai: Best small stories from Aotearoa New Zealand* (Canterbury University Press, 2018).

Amber Moffat is a writer and visual artist from Dunedin who lives in Western Australia. She makes work for both children and adults. Her writing for adults has been published by *Glottis*, *Overland* and Night Parrot Press.

Janet Newman is a poet who won the 2015 New Zealand Poetry Society International Competition, and the 2017 Kathleen Grattan Prize for a Sequence of Poems. She was a runner-up in the 2019 Kathleen Grattan Award. Her first collection is forthcoming from Otago University Press.

Rachel O'Connor's short fiction and nonfiction have been published in Ireland and New Zealand and broadcast on RNZ. Her first novel, *Whispering City* (2015), was recently translated into Greek. While working on her second novel, she is completing a creative PhD at the University of Auckland, where she is also a tutor of literature and creative writing.

Claire Orchard's work has appeared in various journals and anthologies. Her first poetry collection, *Cold Water Cure*, was published by Victoria University Press in 2016.

Joanna Preston is a Tasmanaut poet, editor and freelance creative writing tutor who lives in semi-rural Canterbury. She is learning to speak Zoom.

Chris Price's most recent poetry collection is *Beside Herself* (Auckland University Press, 2016). An essay and collaboration with photographer Bruce Foster is forthcoming in the Kōrero Series (Massey University Press).

Bridget Reweti is an artist and curator from Ngāti Ranginui and Ngāi Te Rangi in Tauranga Moana. She is the 2020–21 Frances Hodgkins Fellow at the University of Otago, co-edits *ATE Journal of Māori Art* and has a collaborative practice with Mata Aho Collective.

Victor Rodger is an award-winning playwright, screenwriter and producer of Samoan (Iva) and Scottish (Dundee) descent. His fiction has been published by *Landfall* and *Verb Wellington*. He was recently named an Officer of the New Zealand Order of Merit for services to theatre and Pacific Arts.

Tim Saunders farms sheep and beef near Palmerston North. He has had poetry and short stories published in *Turbine|Kapohau*, *takahē*, *Landfall*, *Poetry NZ Yearbook* and *Flash Frontier*. He won the 2018 Mindfood Magazine Short Story Competition, and placed third in the 2019 and 2020 National Flash Fiction Day Awards. His memoir *This Farming Life* was published by Allen & Unwin in 2020.

Rebecca Styles has a PhD in creative writing. She has had short stories published in New Zealand journals and anthologies and teaches story writing at Wellington High School Community Education Centre.

Rowan Taigel is a Dunedin poet who can often be found writing poetry in local cafés. She was a finalist in the 2020 Caselberg International Poetry Competition, and her work has been published in *Catalyst*, *takahē*, *Aotearotica*, *A Fine Line*, *Shot Glass Journal* and numerous NZPS anthologies.

Ethan Te Ora (Ngāti Maniapoto, Waikato/Tainui) is a writer, journalist and filmmaker based in Te Whānganui-a-Tara. They won the Modern Letters Creative Nonfiction Prize 2020 for the manuscript of their first book, *Tuakiri*, from which 'Paper Crowns, Bucket Hats' is taken.

Joy Tong is a Kiwi-Asian student and writer based in Tāmaki Makaurau, where she attempts to keep her basil plant alive and pets strangers' cats. Her work can be found in *Starling*, *Mayhem* and *Signals*.

Angela Trolove is a writer and arts reviewer based in Dunedin. She reviews for *Theatreview* NZ. 'Braided Rivers' is an excerpt from her upcoming novel, which received a 2020 NZSA Complete Manuscript Assessment. She is currently working on a collection of short stories.

Aditya Vasudevan is a lawyer working in Sydney who edited the University of Auckland student magazine *Craccum* in 2013 and later contributed a regular column on philosophy and culture.

Helen Watson White has been a high-school and university teacher, library assistant, editor and art photographer, and since 1974 has published theatre, book, music, art and opera reviews, along with articles, short stories, poems and photographs.

Tom Weston's recent collections are *What is Left Behind* (Steele Roberts, 2017), longlisted for the Ockham Book Awards, and *Positano in Fifteen Divertimenti* (Steele Roberts, 2019).

CONTRIBUTIONS

Landfall publishes original poems, essays, short stories, excerpts from works of fiction and non-fiction in progress, reviews, articles on the arts, and portfolios by artists. Submissions must be emailed to landfall@otago.ac.nz with 'Landfall submission' in the subject line.

Visit our website www.otago.ac.nz/press/landfall/index.html for further information.

SUBSCRIPTIONS

Landfall is published in May and November. The subscription rates for 2021 (two issues) are: New Zealand $55 (including GST); Australia $NZ65; rest of the world $NZ70. Sustaining subscriptions help to support New Zealand's longest running journal of arts and letters, and the writers and artists it showcases. These are in two categories: Friend: between $NZ75 and $NZ125 per year. Patron: $NZ250 and above.

Send subscriptions to Otago University Press, PO Box 56, Dunedin, New Zealand. For enquiries, email landfall@otago.ac.nz or call 64 3 479 8807.

Print ISBN: 978-1-99-004801-2
ePDF ISBN: 978-1-99-004802-9
ISSN 00–23–7930

Published by Otago University Press,
533 Castle Street, Dunedin,
New Zealand.

Typeset by Otago University Press.
Printed in New Zealand by Caxton.

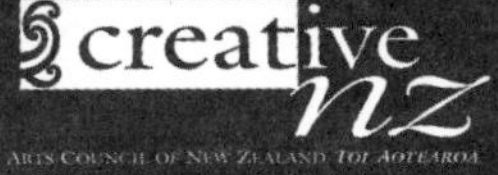

EMPTY

Claire Beynon, *Empty*, 2020, embossed print on Fabriano, 380 x 283mm